Paolo Fusero

E-CITY

DIGITAL NETWORKS AND CITIES OF THE FUTURE

to Gaia

E-CITY

DIGITAL NETWORKS AND CITIES OF THE FUTURE

Paolo Fusero

Appendix edited by E. Morello, A.Biderman, F.M. Rojas, C. Ratti

E-NETWORK

E-PLANNING

E-CITIES

0

INTRO 0

NETWORK
E-PLANNING
E-CITIES

Key to the reading

In writing this book, my aim is to reflect upon the perspectives related to the development of *Information and Communication Technologies* (ICTs) Particularly, I will try to understand whether the innovations deriving from these new technologies can bring about significant changes in urban planning and in future urban models.

The underlying hypothesis is that the field of urban and territorial planning is undergoing a transitional period where new technologies merge with old methodologies of project elaboration. In the academic world, as well as in the public administration, not everyone seems to have fully understood the scope of the "digital revolution", and this translates into a sort of resistance to change.

Nevertheless, new information and communication technologies nowadays permeate all aspects of our social life and are bringing about substantial changes in the way people relate to each other as well as in individual behaviours. The so-called *Digital Life* is a phenomenon that concerns the younger generations in advanced societies: in addition to classroom education, young people learn to develop new codes of human interaction thanks to computers, mobile phones, SMS, the i-pod and all the other digital multimedia tools currently available on the market.

The proliferation of digital applications has already induced radical changes in several sectors. By way of example, we can mention the automation of production processes, photography, financial transactions, home banking and on-line shopping. In addition to that, we can expect new and more user-friendly applications to be developed in the future and to become ordinary tools in our daily lives, thus affecting our habits and determining new life styles.

In the wake of such considerations, the book tries to look at the future. It does so by focusing not really on the technological, sociological or economical aspects of the phenomenon, but rather on the new urban models that will be developed in an information society that is increasingly geared towards globalisation, and on the urban planning tools that will regulate future land transformation processes.

The book is divided in three parts: 1) *e-Network*, which emphasises the development of digital networks and the ensuing land transformation processes; 2) *e-Planning*, which focuses particularly on planning tools and the innovations brought about by the development of ICTs; 3) *e-City*, which looks at the cities and territories of the future. Each part stems from one initial question which underlies and directs the whole reasoning.

PART 1. e-Network

«*Can digital networks determine territorial settlement patterns, thus playing the role which was previously exerted by other network infrastructures, such as the rail or the motorway system?*»

In tackling this issue, we have to bear the following in mind: digital networks have to be viewed as a new category of public works in its own right; thus, we must think of their strategic use in synergy with other public works.

As a matter of fact, contrary to common thinking, digital networks are not "immaterial", but they are conveyed by a physical infrastructure made of pylons, cables, aerials, satellites, hardware and software platforms. Communications systems, which are the physical pillar required to set up a digital network, can be either via cable (twisted pair, optic fibre) or wireless (wiFi, wiMax, UMTS, satellite) and they differ in cost, set-up time and performance, which is not a secondary issue at all. The very rapid evolution of information applications determines an early obsolescence of equipment and services, thus requiring greater processing power (computer) and higher performance telecommunication systems (broadband). It is precisely the availability of broadband networks which is becoming an insufficient though necessary condition for the development and competitiveness of territories. Many on-line services can be used as indicators to determine the level of attractiveness of a specific territory: telemedicine, e-government,

ASP services, but also home banking, e-learning, e-commerce, etc. As an example, let us focus on the services offered to enterprises. Particularly at small and medium enterprise level, we see a consolidation of "outsourced services", i.e. phases of the production process (which are peripheral to the core objective of the company) that are entrusted to external companies in order to reduce costs and ensure adequate qualitative standards. Many of these services can be carried out on-line, provided that a performing telecommunication system is available. This shows that the competitiveness of a territory can be measured according to the availability of digital networks suited to the new needs of companies and citizens. And this may sometimes conflict with the policies of broadband development adopted in various countries. In this early phase, the creation of infrastructures for telecommunication systems was completely left in the hands of private operators who, quite rightly from their point of view, followed a market-oriented approach. The result was a reasonable acceleration in the distribution of ADSL technology (the first step into the world of broadband communication), but a limited achievement, for instance, of optic fibre networks in a few big cities, where the service area ensured an economic return on the wiring costs incurred by the private operator.

This should make us reflect upon the Digital Divide phenomenon which, to the mind of many people, boiled down to southern countries being opposed to more developed ones. As a matter of fact, within some European countries it is also possible to measure a considerable gap in the competitiveness between those territories which are reached by robust digital networks and those which are cut-off from them, such as rural and mountainous areas. It is likely that this divide will become even greater as the increase in traffic and the development of ICT applications provided through digital networks will require even "broader" bands and the twisted pair will no longer be sufficient for the provision of the service. ADSL 4Mb/sec (the most commonly used in our households) was the fastest connection speed a few years ago, but is already inadequate for several types of services. We see it, when we want to watch a movie in streaming[1] or when we want to start a video-conference.

This train of thought leads us to a conclusion: it is most likely high time to start a second phase of digital network development, characterised by a closer public-private relationship to ensure the management and rationalisation of network infrastructures and on-line services. Public

[1] The term *streaming* refers to a flow of audio/video data transmitted by a source to one or more destinations through a telematic network. The data are decompressed and reproduced a few seconds after their reception has begun, without the need to download the entire original file in order to be able to use it.

authorities can no longer "gaze out the window" letting commercial factors be the only ones to determine the development of digital networks. They must, on the contrary, perform their duty and set out an overall strategy which combines the legitimate economic objectives of private operators with the development policies of various territorial contexts. To this end, the digital network must be considered as a truly strategic objective, just like the other network infrastructures. This is what determines the great value of digital networks in their interpretation as a new category of public works.

In the first part of the book, we try to piece together the role of infrastructure networks in the development of western civilization (chap. 1), from Roman ancient networks to modern Trans-European Networks. What emerges is a direct link between the development of network infrastructures and the development of the economy. It may be difficult to determine which one comes first, but there is certainly a symbiotic relationship. The future will bring us global networks, further investments and, above all, new relationships between the public and the private sectors (chap. 2). The traditional sources of financing for infrastructural networks (state budgets) will inevitably disappear because of the physiological ageing of the population, the resulting curtailed tax revenue and the greater attention paid to other aspects, such as welfare, social security, tax pressure, environmental protection, etc. All this suggests that, in the near future, public financial resources might not be sufficient to accomplish and maintain the infrastructural networks required by more industrialised countries, and that resorting to public-private partnerships might therefore be appropriate. Any consideration on the future of infrastructural networks cannot disregard climate change and global warming. This is why we have used four different scenarios (chap.3) to simulate how some events in conjunction with some scientific discoveries and social changes can determine the future of our planet. We then tried to understand the environmental, social and economic implications of each simulated scenario. The resulting considerations underline the importance of scientific research applied to infrastructural networks and, more generally, to production processes, in order to optimise performance and reduce consumption. From a physical point of view, future "intelligent" infrastructural systems will not differ considerably from the current ones. The differences will lie in the way they will be able to react to external input and in the services they will able to provide to end-users. As a conclusion to the first part of the book (chap.4), we will dwell upon a particular category of infrastructural networks, the digital networks, and we will describe their evolution from their dawn to the new economy, focusing on the effects on modern society.

PART 2. e-Planning

«Can the widespread use of ICT technologies contribute to the innovation of projects for territorial and urban transformation?»

The second part of the book deals with the innovation of urban tools (chap.5). There has been a lot of debate in the past about the possibility that the techniques that lead to the elaboration of tools could actually induce substantial changes in terms of their contents. No doubt, the recent ICT innovations have found interesting applications in the urban sector, such as the *GIS (Geographical Information System)* or e-Government. However, the overall impression is that these substantial changes in urban planning tools induced by new technologies are limited to the representation of cities and territories (CAD and 3D modelling) and to knowledge acquisition processes (relational databases and GIS). Very little, in fact, have they contributed to the processes involved in the communication of choices and, even less, to the decision-making processes involved in the elaboration and management of solutions.

When talking about Digital Urban Planning[2], even those who are most sensitive to the issue refer to the rationalisation and development of network infrastructures and to the on-line services that can be provided on the territory by those networks. Needless to say, they intend to demonstrate that networking is essential for the social organisation of the city of the future[3]. However, translating their thoughts into urban planning tools that are truly capable of regulating territorial transformations by making the most out of ICT yet requires a lot of daring. A group of Chinese scholars have been busy carrying out some undoubtedly interesting research on the concept of Digital Urban Planning[4]. The expression "Digital Planning" is also starting to arouse a certain degree of interest among the national scientific community[5] and some local authorities have embarked on some initial experiments in this regard[6]. We should try to understand the state of the art and the new perspectives for Digital Urban Planning (chap. 6), meaning the innovations that recent technologies in conjunction with the use of internet can induce on urban techniques, on tool production methodologies and on territorial governance procedures.

An additional remark is required for the question introducing the second part of the book (the equation ICT = tools innovation). Three different phases can be identified in a territorial transformation project:

(2) see Wu S. et al., "Digital Urban Planning, Concept and support technology", in Lai M. and Wang M., *Theory and Practice of Digital City*, World Book Press, Guangzhou 2001.
(3) see. Castells M., "La città delle reti", Marsilio, Venice 2004. *(The city of networks)*
(4) see. Anrong Dang, Huizhen S., Haoying H., Lei W., "Study on system of technical methods for digital urban planning", ISPRS Workshop on Service and Application of Data Infrastructure, XXXVI (4/W6), October 14-16, Hangzhou, China 2005.

knowledge acquisition, decision-making, implementation and effect monitoring. Applied to an urban plan, the first phase corresponds to urban analyses and their representation; the second phase to the elaboration of Plan Tables and of implementation technical norms; the third phase to the approval and management of the plan.

The knowledge acquisition phase is perhaps the most impacted by technological innovations in the planning process. It embraces new representation methodologies (bi-dimensional and tri-dimensional) as well as new digital technologies that support territorial analyses: satellite pictures using Google earth, bird's eye representations using Live search, data on traffic and pollution collected by detection stations, etc. Technological platforms used to achieve additional levels of knowledge on the territory, such as the GIS, can also be assimilated to this phase. From a telematic perspective, e-government services are also innovative tools that can be used to carry out administrative activities and, at the same time, increase the level of knowledge on the territory.

The decision-making phase is more empirical and the borderline with political mediation is more blurred. This is also why, up to now, new

(5) see. Fistola R., "Nuovi strumenti urbanistici per il governo delle trasformazioni territoriali indotte dalle nuove tecnologie della comunicazione: il Piano Digitale", XXII Italian Conference on regional Science, AISRE, Venice October 2001. (New urban planning tools for the management of territorial transformations brought about by new communication technologies: the Digital Plan)
(6) see Fistola R., "Digital urban planning e pianificazione digitale del territorio", XXVII Italian Conference on Regional Science, AISRE, Pisa October 2006. In this paper, the author presents the Digital Plan for the city of Benevento, Campania.

technologies have had a more feeble impact. Yet, we can observe some evident improvements, for instance, in the possibility to contribute to the choices being made. NIMBY[7] phenomena, which often retard or even hinder the achievement of important projects of public works, can be kept within physiological limits by applying suitable information sharing methodologies and by promoting participation to decision-making processes thanks to the internet. The internet can be an amazing tool for the support of democratic participation to the political debate. Its added-value lies in the fact that, while providing institutions and political associations with an extraordinary tool to disseminate information among citizens, it also activates the opposite process, by enabling citizens to participate to the political debate and to the shaping of tendencies and orientations, at both institutional and party levels. Furthermore, internet is perceived by users as a more credible and trustworthy tool than other communication means, since it does not pass through any filters.

The implementation and monitoring phase has always been the Achilles' heel of urban planning. Innovative projects with a clear scientific value can be nullified during the approval process and remain entangled in the warp of management procedures which do not allow for any changes unless through the painstaking "Institute of Variation". In this field, suggestions for a more productive use of new technologies are less frequent: it is clearly yet an experimental phase. We can only point to general objectives for increased flexibility. For instance, we could make the Technical Norms for the Implementation of Plans more suited to the achievement of established public service provision objectives. We could elaborate performance-based fabricability indexes according to the energy-efficiency level of buildings. Or we could resort to equalisation models that are based on permutation processes managed by a GIS which is capable of indicating the availability of suitable parcels and the interests of building plots' owners in these permutational operations.

PART 3. e-City

«*Can the widespread use of digital networks, in the long term, give rise to new urban models or even new land management schemes?*»

The third part of the book focuses on the future of our cities and our territories with respect to the development of digital networks and to the increasingly common use of ICT applications. The concept of digital cities is becoming increasingly integrated into the common language, conjuring up science fiction scenarios of cities that are more

(7t) The acronym NIMBY *(Not In My Back Yard)* indicates an attitude of protest against works of public interest which are deemed necessary, but are not wanted in one's own territory. Typical examples are the construction of important communication axes, waste-to-energy plants, landfills, roma camps, power plants, etc.

and more projected towards the future. However, if we look for a more accurate definition using, for example, an internet search engine, we find out that this expression can have different meanings. The concept of Digital Cities is often associated with an arena where people from a local community can interact with each other and exchange knowledge, experiences, services or simply share interests using the internet[8]. This is, for example, the nature of the *American On Line* (AOL) *Digital Cities*. These are on-line guides of the major American cities where, besides comprehensive information on entertainment and tourist activities (restaurants, attractions, cinemas, etc.), the user has the possibility to purchase services and products on-line. More complex are experiences like the *Amsterdam Digital City*, which appears like a hardware/software platform allowing citizens to interact with the public administration in order to obtain services or information, using the PC at home, or from other locations in public areas (libraries, bus stops, etc.[9]. The *Helsinki Arena Project* is even more diverse. It creates a virtual city using a 3D model and allows for the interaction of citizens through *live video*[10].

The *Kyoto Digital City* is a complex architecture on three layers which is capable of creating synergies and providing citizens and tourists with a lot of information and services obtained from the GIS such as, for example, real time data collected by detection centres scattered throughout the city (traffic, parking capacity, weather, pollution, etc.)[11].

All these experiences (and many others which have not been mentioned but are just as meaningful) have a common denominator: the Digital City is conceived as a more or less complex user-friendly hardware/software architecture, which is more or less rich in terms of interaction possibilities and provides information and services to the citizen-user with regard to different areas, such as tourism, trade, transport, welfare, health, civil protection, politics, etc.

Although innovative, the different meanings of the *Digital City* that we have so far analysed and the pilot projects on which they are based are solely limited to the technical aspects of the hardware/software platforms that convey them: Digital City = Virtual City. In other words, the city, its functions and, where possible, its interactions are simply represented in a virtual arena created through ICTs. Quite interesting, but certainly well below our objectives! We are more interested in expanding the concept of Digital City and associate it with a city of the future where the intensive use of ICTs can produce considerable

(8) see Ishida T., "Understanding Digital Cities: Cross-Cultural Perspectives", MIT Press, Cambridge, MA, 2002.
(9) see Van den Besselaar P. and Beckers D., "Demographics and Sociographics of the Digital City", Springer-Verlag, New York, 1998.
(10) see Linturi R., Koivunen M. and Sulkanen J., "Helsinki Arena 2000: augmenting a real city to a virtual one", in Digital Cities: Experiences, Technologies and Future Perspectives, Springer Verlag, New York, 2000.
(11) see Ishida T., "Digital City Kyoto", in Communications of the ACM, n. 7 vol.45, July 2002.

changes in the way in which the city is used, and perhaps even change its spatial organisation.

In this branch of research, some key authors are William J. Mitchell[12] and Manuel Castells[13], who have made, over the past few years, important considerations on the sociological effects of a future dominated by ICTs. Following the reasoning of these two authors, let us try to foresee the consequences of the "digital revolution" on the future of our cities (chap. 7). We realise that we are faced with a complex phenomenon of fragmentation and reassembling of existing urban models. A bit like in a chemical reaction, where some links are broken up, others are preserved, and new chemical components of unknown properties are created *ex novo*[14]. It is unlikely that these transformations will happen in a sudden and catastrophic manner. On the contrary, they will take place in a slow and incremental way. Particularly interesting for us in this process are the new relations that can be established between new urban models and the perspectives of environmental, social and economic sustainability. We have started to ponder on a new concept, that of "digital ecology", which can actually represent a new frontier for sustainable development. Whereas during the economic boom of the industrial era, important aesthetic, environmental and cultural values were often sacrificed in the name of development, the new information society, characterised by a new sensitivity towards these issues, imposes different choices. The digital era can mark the reapproaching of man and the environment, through a sustainable use of its resources thanks to scientific innovations, among other things. In a society which is increasingly service-oriented, the use of information and communication technologies can no longer be viewed as an optional. On the contrary, it is an indispensable prerequisite for sustainable development and for the competitiveness of territories, especially the ones which have remained on the fringes of global development (chap. 8).

(12) see Mitchell, William J., "City of Bits: Space, Place and the Infobahn" (MIT Press, 1995); "E-topia: Urban Life, Jim – But Not As We Know It" (MIT Press, 1999); "Me ++: The Cyborg Self and the Networked City" (MIT Press, 2003).
(13) see Castells M., "The Information Society and the Welfare State: The Finnish Model", Oxford UP, Oxford 2002; "The Network Society: A Cross-Cultural Perspective", Cheltenham, UK; Northampton, MA, Edward Edgar 2004; "The Network Society: From Knowledge to Policy", Center for Transatlantic Relations 2006.
(14) see Mitchell, William J., "Designing the Digital City", in: AAVV, *Digital City*, Springer Berlin, Berlin 2000.

At the end of the book, the reader will find an appendix which summarises some recent studies carried out by the *Senseable City Lab of the Massachusetts Institute of Technology*, Boston. This in-depth analysis is particularly interesting because it walks us through the frontiers of innovation, as they have been traced by researchers at the MIT in their description, understanding and planning of future cities.

The Senseable City Lab is a research group at the MIT, somewhere between the "Media Lab" and the department of "Urban Studies and Planning", which set out to understand how new technologies can change the way in which we study, use and plan the city. It has three main research fields:

1) The first one concerns the use of new technologies to describe and understand the city. An example could be an extensively widespread technology such as mobile telephony. By mapping the intensity of the radio signals received by aerials, according to both geographical and time-related criteria (hour of the day, day of the week), we can reconstruct some patterns of urban space use, such as the movements of people or the origin-destination of traffic flows. Such descriptions can help us better understand the functioning of cities, by identifying criticalities of the system, places and hours prone to bottlenecks, crowded areas, etc.

2) The second research field concerns man-computer interfaces allowing for planning operations to be better adapted to the potential of new technologies. For instance, by trying to mend the separation between the use of CAD for drawing and numerical checks and the use of 3D modelling tools to verify spatial components and assess the impact of planned elements on the surrounding environment.

3) The third research field tries to understand how new technologies can change the physical aspect of cities, for instance, by using new materials to turn the façades of a skyscraper into huge digital displays. Today, in Times Square, every building is actually already a display, but currently used technologies are faced with a serious limitation: these buildings have no natural light, no natural ventilation and no views to the outside.

Research on new materials could lead to the use of special glass surfaces allowing for an external view from the inside, and making it possible to visualize writings, information or any other type of media from the outside, thanks to different levels of transparency.

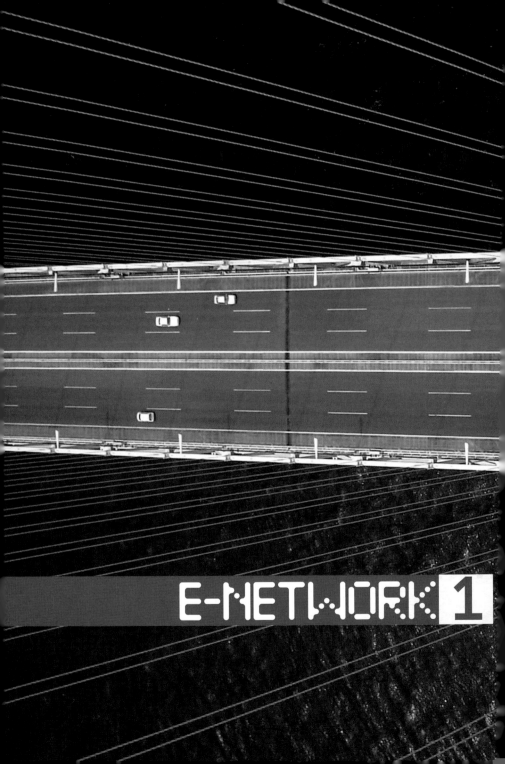

E-NETWORK 1

1. Network-based civilisations

1.1 Ancient networks

Since the dawn of our civilisation, we have provided ourselves with infrastructural networking systems which have profoundly affected our development. Let us focus on ancient networks, such as the aqueducts or the road systems built by the Romans. They were built for military, political and economic purposes, but in the end they affected the development of entire regions in Europe and in the Mediterranean area. In the beginning, they were named after the city to which they led (via "Ardeatina") or after the people that they reached (via "Latina"). Or sometimes they bore the name of the function they were conceived for (via "Salaria"). From the IV cen. BC onwards, new important roads leading to far-away regions started to be built and they were named after the consuls that had achieved them (i.e. via "Appia" initiated by Appius Claudius Caecus to open a way to the Magna Graecia during the Samnitic Wars). The great Roman consular roads (*vie consolari*), which were originally conceived for specific military strategies, were not restricted to this objective, but became an important conveyer of civilisation, by facilitating the circulation of goods, merchants, messengers, ordinary people and by fostering economic interactions and cultural exchanges among people. The ancient territory thus started to change its set-up: the exclusively natural landscape, which had been a characterising feature for millennia, started to be complemented by a man-made dimension that would grow stronger and stronger over succeeding periods. By measuring distances and, consequently, the time required to cover them, milestones gave increasingly defined contours to vast territories. In practice, Roman roads enabled a network of political, economic and social relations which played a fundamental role in the development of European and Mediterranean civilisations.
In the history of our continent, another important period was characterised by the capital role played by infrastructural networks in transforming the territory and developing new urban models: the *Industrial Revolution*[15]. It was a sudden development of the technologies applied to industrial production which originated in England towards the second half of the 18th century. The first significant consequence of the industrial revolution was the demographic increase: in Great Britain the population rose from 6.5 million inhabitants in 1750 to 14 million in 1831[16]. The distribution of the population over the territory changed considerably: the countryside was progressively depopulated and citizens settled massively around urban agglomerations, which expanded in a rapid and chaotic way. The organisation of work was also subject

[15] see L. Benevolo, "Le origini dell'urbanistica moderna", Laterza, Bari, 1984. (*The origins of modern urbanism*)
[16] see C. Barbagallo, "Le origini della grande industria contemporanea", Florence 1951. (*The origins of the great contemporary industry*)

1. Roman Aqueduct (Segovia)   2. Ancient Appian Way (Rome)

3. Forgaria Bridge (Udine)   4. Paderno d'Adda Bridge (Lecco)

to changes. The model of the family-run business, which was previously spread throughout the territory, was now replaced by industrial production concentrated in big factories that were initially built in the proximity of water courses and later moved close to coal mines[17] The development of goods production, fuelled by the new mechanical technologies, led to the fast saturation of existing markets and to the consequent need to find new outlets. In order to increase capital, transport networks had to be improved. This is why during the 19th century, under the lead of England, France and Germany, Europe witnessed the progressive achievement of new infrastructural networks: canals, roads, railways, bridges, harbours. The bumpy English parish streets of the 17th century, maintained thanks to the unremunerated work of citizens (the *corvé*), were now replaced by modern toll roads built by private companies using innovative techniques[18]. Estuaries and rivers were interconnected through a web of navigable canals. The invention of the steam locomotive by Stephenson marked the development of the railway network, which was initially privately owned, and then publicly managed.

Thus, while some utopians (Owen, Fourier, Godin, etc.) took great pains with the elaboration of proposals for new urban models capable of responding to the crisis of the industrial city, while Marx and Engels promoted the political organisation of the proletariat and theorised

(17) see T.S. Ashthon, "La rivoluzione industriale", Bari 1953, pp. 5-7. (*The industrial revolution*)
(18) For instance, the roads built using the technological innovations introduced by the patents of two engineers, Mr Mc Adam and Mr Telford, were highly widespread.

a profound transformation of the capitalistic system, a whole generation of functionalist technicians were busy transforming the city and the territory through the achievement of modern infrastructural networks that changed completely the European territorial set-up and induced new urban models. New cities were created in the proximity of networks and the ancient medieval cities built at the top of high hills for defensive purposes were doomed to a slow decline because of their distance from new transport networks.

1.2 Modern networks

In Italy the realisation of infrastructural networks and, more generally, the industrialisation process have been slow and difficult, for several reasons. Up until 1861, Italy was fragmented into a multitude of small states; a strict customs regime imposed heavy taxes on the transport of goods; unlike England, Belgium or France Italy had no iron or coal reserves; the peculiar territorial morphology impeded communication (Alps, Apennines); the construction of roads or railways was therefore complex and costly. The decision to privilege the development of road networks (and implicitly private transport over public transport) was made after the Second World War, when the inadequacy of the railway system in the face of new development needs was finally acknowledged. In the fifties, Italy was still a predominantly rural country and a complete renewal of its productive system was required for its modernisation. Until then, the old minor road system had helped keep rural settlements together and had allowed for sporadic contacts with neighbouring communities and for the exchange of goods over short distances. Everything changed when the economic development determined specific performance needs in the transport sector: new factories required an efficient road network allowing for rapid procurement and rapid positioning of goods on the markets. The demand in the transport sector diversified itself: in addition to goods, the transport of people, both for work and for leisure, acquired greater importance. A new grassroots demand started to take shape for faster individual travel modalities, for private ownership of means of transport, and therefore for a new road network conceived to favour circulation. New economic and industrial hegemonies came into being and great power was acquired by large northern automobile producers, who were capable of having considerable influence on the political decisions made in the field of transport. The automobile industry determined new needs by marketing "passengers cars", i.e. cars which could be afforded by an increasing number of users. Those are the years of *Fiat 600*, *Fiat*

500, *Vespa* and *Lambretta*, the economic boom of the early sixties. The purchase of private cars and the realisation of motorway networks acquired a particular ideological meaning which went well beyond sheer economic considerations: it was a true life style "revolution" in a society that had risen itself from the ashes of the war and looked at the future with renewed optimism[19]. As regards to current development policies for European transport networks, the Maastricht Treaty of 1992 played a decisive role. Its priorities were the rationalisation and improvement of connections between member States in order to facilitate the circulation of goods, people and ideas, and try to plug the major gaps ("bottlenecks" and missing connections) in the three big categories of networks identified: transport, energy and telecommunications. The *Trans-European Transport Networks* (TEN-T) include strategic projects for road transport, waterways and maritime harbours, airways and airports, as well as the European network for high-speed trains. The *Trans-European Energy Networks* (TEN-E) concern electricity and natural gas. The *Trans-European Telecommunications Networks* (e-TEN) aim at developing electronic services based on telecommunication networks. Despite the great difficulties faced by these projects in their implementation phase, hindered by various problems related to the availability of funds and local policies, it is clear that the strategic axes identified by the TEN networks will represent in the long run the backbone for the future development of Europe. Particularly noteworthy is the importance given, within this strategic development framework, to immaterial networks: energy and telecommunications. For the first time, broadband networks, global satellite navigation systems (Galileo[20]) and multimedia applications are put on an equal footing with transport infrastructure networks in terms of their ability to generate new territorial spatial dimensions.

(19) see Anna Lamberti, "Le strade in Italia: dalle origini all'autostrada del Sole", (*Italian roads: from the origins to the Autostrada del Sole*) working paper published on http://cronologia. leonardo.it

(20) Galileo is a global satellite navigation system for civil use which is part of one of the strategic actions provided for by the TEN networks. Once fully completed, the system will consist of a set of 30 satellites associated with the necessary terrestrial infrastructures that will be able to function on a multitude of applications. It will provide a considerably higher level of accuracy than that which is currently available with the GPS system: from strictly transport-related sectors (air, maritime, rail, road) to communications, from agricultural policies to civil protection systems and territorial mapping, and so forth.

2. New horizons

2.1 Global networks

The economic effects of the development of infrastructural networks have been a subject of studies since the early eighties. Although it is possible to identify a direct link between the development of network infrastructures and economic development, it is not easy to establish which one comes first. Can the development of infrastructures fuel the economy? Or is it rather the opposite? Researchers in the field of economy essentially seem to agree that public investments in the infrastructure sector have had a less visible return than what was originally foreseen by their colleagues thirty years ago[21].

It has been demonstrated that the efficiency and profitability of infrastructural networks is only partially dependent upon the investments made for their realisation. A capital role is played by the nature of the investments and their ability to create synergies with other infrastructural networks, in other words, by their ability to create *Networks*.

The telecommunications sector is perhaps the network infrastructure that offers the greatest development and innovation possibilities in the short-medium term, in terms of service improvement and cost reduction. Let us take VoIP[22] as an example, or RFID[23] applications, or the optic fibre and all the services that it can convey, or mobile telephony, or component miniaturisation, or the civil use of satellite technologies, etc.

The spectrum of innovation possibilities in these sectors is so wide that it is difficult to even elaborate reliable future scenarios about what will happen in more than twenty years time.

On the other hand, in the road transport sector, technological innovations are likely to have a weaker impact on future scenarios.

As things stand now, no technological revolution could substantially change transport modalities in the course of the next 30 years. High-speed trains are already in place.

The equipment and monitoring systems will probably be improved, but there will be no technological innovation capable of revolutionising the system.

There will always be an electric traction engine towing a certain number of wagons. Regarding other transport systems, by road or by sea, it is likely that in the near future new developments will result in more efficient equipment capable of reducing consumption and using alternative fuels instead of oil. It is also likely that design innovations will improve fluid dynamic penetration efficiency and that automated

(21) see Stevens B., Shieb P.A., Andrieu M., "A cross-sectoral perspective on the development of global infrastructures to 2030" in *Infrastructure to 2030*, OCDE ed., Paris 2006.
(22) Voice over IP (voice over Internet Protocol) is a technology which makes it possible to deliver a telephone communication using an internet connection or a different dedicated network that uses the IP protocol rather than a traditional telephone network.
(23) RFID (*Radio Frequency IDentification*) is a technology for the automatic identification of objects, animals or people. The system is based on the remote reading of the information contained in a microchip.

driving assistance systems will actually increase the level of safety, but it is unlikely that these types of infrastructural networks will be turned upside down in the short-medium term.

Conversely, new technologies may play a determining role in the future of infrastructural networks involved in water supply and manure disposal.

Firstly, ICT innovations together with modern spatial technologies will increase the ability to monitor all aspects of water supply on a global scale. Secondly, biotechnologies will significantly innovate pollution prevention and monitoring systems, thus revolutionising water treatment processes.

Current treatment plants will inevitably be replaced in the near future by new systems based on innovative purification methodologies which could even eliminate the distinction between distribution and disposal plants, as they could then be combined in one process.

Finally, water distribution networks will also improve their performance thanks to the innovations in the field of nanotechnologies, which will produce specific sensors capable of perfecting network monitoring procedures and of exploiting the self-regeneration properties of new "intelligent" materials[24].

[24] Stevens B., Shieb P.A., Andrieu M., op.cit.
[25] Source: OECD Statistic 2008, Organisation for Economic Co-Operation and Development, www.sourceoecd.org

2.2 Future investments

On a global scale, it is estimated that overall investments in the field of network infrastructures will increase from 650 billion dollars per year in 2005 to 745 billion dollars in 2010, but they will then go down to 646 billion dollars in 2015, to 572 in 2020 and 171 in 2025[25]. After an initial increase, the rather sensitive reduction foreseen for the end of the next twenty-year period is due, according to the *Organisation for Economic Co-Operation and Development*[26], to the progressive commitment to operations of maintenance and adjustment of existing networks and to the consequent slowing down in the realisation of new network sections.

The overall expenditure required to maintain existing networks at their level of functionality is estimated to represent 80% of the total in 2010 and more than 90% in 2020.

For the next 30 years, the ex novo construction of new network infrastructures will primarily regard the telecommunications sector, particularly optic fibre and radio networks. The development of mobile communication will absorb the majority of total investments, whilst the realisation of fixed networks will play a complementary role in the system and will be mostly used for long distance connections.

According to the OECD, the economic growth of developing countries over the next twenty years and the resulting new connectivity needs will considerably boost the development of digital networks: according to estimates, there will be 3.5 billion potential users against the current 2 billion.

In the coming twenty years, investments will also increase in the energy sector, primarily for the maintenance of existing plants and networks. For this specific sector, it might be useful to imagine two different possible scenarios.

The first scenario is based on the assumption that global energy policies will not considerably divert from the current line. In this case, according to the OECD, global investments until 2030 can be estimated at about 350 billion dollars per year, and around half of them (53%) will be used for energy distribution. The major percentage of investments (60%) will concern the development of production and distribution networks in developing countries, particularly China, whilst industrialised countries will mainly use their resources for the maintenance of existing networks.

The second scenario takes into account the impact of new global energy policies targeted at reducing consumption and introducing al-

(26) The OECD (*Organisation for Economic Co-operation and Development*) is an International organisation uniting the most developed countries in order to promote forms of economic and financial cooperation. Beside Northern American and European States (excluding the Balkans), it includes Australia, New Zealand, Japan and South Korea.

ternative sources of energy and renewables. In this case, the demand for new investments in the energy sector in industrialised countries should grow less rapidly than in the previous scenario and should lead, for the same period of time, to a reduction by 15%.

In surface transport, we can indentify two components: on wheel and on rail.

As for wheel transport, statistical forecasts elaborated by the OECD estimate yearly investments between 220 and 290 billion dollars for the period 2005-2030, which will be mainly used for the maintenance and repair of existing infrastructures. As for rail transport, current forecasts estimate yearly investments between 50 and 60 billion dollars for the period 2005-2030. These amounts are much higher than the forecasts contained in some economic studies twenty years ago. This is due to the proactive impetus given by the European TEN-T programme to the realisation of high-speed train networks in economically developed countries and to the realisation of new main railway lines in developing countries, especially China. Besides these forecasts, worldwide policies in this sector show a clear tendency to deviate a yearly amount of 20-30 billion dollars worth of funding from road to rail traffic.

In the field of water supply and distribution, the OECD estimates that yearly investments will be as much as 770 billion dollars by 2015 or even exceed 1,000 billion dollars by 2025.

In Europe and the US, most of these investments will be used for the maintenance and functional adjustment of existing networks, rather than for the construction of new systems, given the fact that water networks in industrialised countries are generally quite old and badly preserved.

Constructing new water systems is necessary, however, in developing countries: in Africa, only 40% of the population has access to an adequate water network; in Latin America, in the Caribbean, in Asia and in the Pacific Islands, the percentage goes up to 80%, but is still largely insufficient for the needs of the population.

In more industrialised countries, increasing the level of investments in the water sector will mostly depend on the political pressure exerted by public opinion, which is becoming increasingly concerned with environmental issues.

The future of water resources will be at the centre of the political debate, not only because, like food and air, it is indispensable for life on earth, but also because worldwide investments in this field (and

the consequent water "business") are bound to grow more than in any other infrastructural sector in the long-term.

The following table gives us a comprehensive picture of the global investment forecasts for the different infrastructural sectors. The data provided by the OECD are rather clear: in the coming decades the sectors of telecommunications (short-middle term) and water supply and distribution (middle-long term) will have the most determining influence on the global political agenda. They will attract resources and determine new economies.

Besides highlighting the importance of telecommunications and water distribution networks, the table gives an overall picture of the rela-

Estimates of yearly global investments in the different infrastructural sectors
Source OECD Statistics 2008, absolute value in billion US dollars

	2000-2010	% world GDP	2010-2020	% world GDP	2020-2030	% world GDP
Roads	220	0,38 %	245	0,32 %	292	0,29 %
Rail	49	0,09 %	54	0,07 %	58	0,06 %
Telecommunications[1]	654	1,14 %	646	0,85 %	171	0,17 %
Electricity[2]	127	0,22 %	180	0,24 %	241	0,24 %
Water[3]	576	1,01 %	772	1,01 %	1.037	1,03 %

(1) Estimates concerning 2005, 2015 and 2025
(2) Taking into account distribution only
(3) 1.Concerning OECD countries, Russia, China, India and Brazil

tive weight that the various sectors are bound to have in the coming decades. Annual investments in the five sectors analysed amount to 2.5% of the GDP[27]. If we also include the production of energy through traditional sources (oil, natural gas, carbon) the total amount rises to 3.5%. The financial resources invested in infrastructural networks during the period 2000-2030 amount to a total of 53,000 billion dollars; if we also consider the production of electricity, the total amount rises to 65,000 billion dollars; and if we take into account the production of energy through traditional sources, the total goes up to 71,000 billion dollars. Needless to say, the amount would be even higher if, besides the different networks, we also considered investments in specific categories of infrastructure: harbours, airports, stations, storage plants, logistic platforms, etc.

The current situation induces OECD countries to direct their priority investments to the maintenance and modernisation of existing networks rather than their expansion. Nonetheless, expenses are estimated to increase considerably partially due to "externalities", such as land price increase, extra costs deriving from new environmental rules, increased planning complexity, etc. In the middle term, all these factors could result in the need to change substantially the financial organisation of infrastructural systems. Unless financial markets are thoroughly reviewed, it is still unclear how the most developed countries will bear the huge costs required to maintain their infrastructural networks at a certain level of efficiency in the coming decades, with the exception perhaps of the telecommunication sector, where the private component is more visible.

We have just outlined the general picture of worldwide investments and the deriving potential elements of uncertainty, which should be viewed in a global context, encompassing the whole planet. We know, however, that economic policies and market strategies can vary, even considerably, from one country to another and, sometimes, also within a country. In Italy, for instance, we see considerable infrastructural differences between the North and the South. At the same time, change can also be determined by scientific advances and by the changing users' needs in a global context. The growing global competition in trade and in the service sector goes hand in hand with an increasing need to be equipped with modern and efficient infrastructural networks for water supply, telecommunications, transport and energy. Core hubs are often inward or outward connecting points: harbours, airports, border entries and the interconnecting rail and road axes. In addition

(27) The GDP - *Gross Domestic Product* – is the overall value of the goods and services produced within a Country in a specific time interval (usually one year). The GDP is one of the parameters used to measure the wealth produced in a Country.

to that, the increasing global energy demand and the dependency of most western nations on foreign countries also play a crucial role, causing some concern as to the cost stability and continuity of supply. As a result of such situation, the role of infrastructural networks in supporting the economic foundations of western civilisations is bound to increase even further in the coming decades, just like the mutual interdependence of various infrastructural networks. This means that the weakness of a network could impair the potential growth of another network. The matrix below briefly illustrates the major synergies between infrastructural sectors that will be further consolidated in the coming decades.

Matrix of interdependence between infrastructural networks
Source OCDE Statistic 2008

	Telecommunications	Electrical network	Transport network	Water network
Telecommunications		Intelligent networks capable of controlling demand through the remote monitoring of meters. Greater market monitoring	Reduced mobility requirements thanks to remotely performed activities such as teleworking, on-line shopping, video-conferences, telemedicine. Improved efficiency in the control of automatic vehicles. Intelligent road systems capable of increasing security and information on traffic. Faster intervention in case of accidents. Telematic markets capable of optimising supply and reducing traffic and travel requirements.	Monitoring of polluting agents and of network maintenance through ICT sensors. Security mechanisms capable of handling the increased vulnerability of systems.
Power supply network	Dependency on power supply. Vulnerability to power cuts. Power supply networks can be used as data transmission cables.		Main source of energy for the rail network. Progress in the development of electric batteries technologies. Use of electric or hybrid vehicles, which increases the need for a network of power filling stations. More urbanised territory means increased ramification of the power supply network and requires greater mobility. Increased costs if road infrastructures intersect underground power supply networks.	Water distribution networks that depend on the availability of electrical energy. Hydropower plants.
Transports network	Increase in the demand of mobile communication, satellite navigation, emergency, control and monitoring services. Information to travellers.	Use of trains for the transport of fuel used to produce energy (coal, oil, gasoline). Increased use of trains for the transport of goods. Increased need for electric power.		Water distribution networks which are often constructed along motorway axes. Improved accessibility thanks to transportation means entails an increased demand of water supply. In the event of an emergency, drinking water is transported by wheeled vehicles through the road network.
Water network	New urbanised areas and new ramifications in the water distribution network increase the demand of telecommunications.	New urbanised areas and new ramifications in the water distribution network increase the demand of electric power.	Waterways which are an alternative to road or rail transport. Increased costs if roads intersect channels or other water system infrastructures.	

2.3 Public-private relationship

The construction of efficient infrastructural networks is not an end in itself, but rather a means through which society tries to ensure a level of welfare adapted to its needs. We have seen that the proper functioning of infrastructural networks depends on their ability to create synergies between them, as well as interdependence and complementarity, and that investments in the coming decades will be conspicuous and diversified in the different sectors.

Traditional financing sources, i.e. state budgets, are doomed to disappear due to the physiological ageing of the population (and the consequent reduced tax income) and the increasing political focus on other issues, such as welfare, social security, reduction of the tax burden, environmental protection etc.

This might suggest that public financial resources may no longer be sufficient for the construction and maintenance of the infrastructural networks required for the development of more industrialised countries.

The data regarding OEDC countries show that public expenditure on fixed capital formation has taken a negative turn, decreasing from 9.5% in 1990 to 7% in 2005.

In the meantime, forecasts for health care assistance estimate an increase from 6.7% of the GDP to 10.1-12.8% by 2050. Moreover, the expenditure related to pension schemes could also increase (within the same timeframe) by 3-4 points on average.

The severity of the impact of such a situation will depend on many factors, such as labour market trends, participation rates, migra-

General Government Gross Fixed Capital Formation (GFCF)
as % of total government outlays average for all OECD countries
Source OECD Statistic 2008

Value of Privatisation Infrastructure Transactions
as % of the total value of privatisation transactions, 1990-2006
Source OCSE Statistic 2008

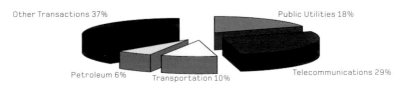

Other Transactions 37%

Public Utilities 18%

Petroleum 6%

Transportation 10%

Telecommunications 29%

tion policies, etc. But it is clear that tax-based public budgets will no longer be capable of satisfying the need for investment in different infrastructural sectors. Therefore, greater recourse to the private sphere and increasingly diversified entries in the public sector will become a necessity.

Nowadays, a significant part of infrastructural networks is already in the hands of private stakeholders, such as telecommunications and, to a lesser extent, power production installations and high-speed train networks.

In the future, in order to be able to face competition from emerging economies in an adequate way, western governments will have to find new sources of capital by creating partnerships with the private sector.

They will have to foster the emergence of new business and development models, including those based on new technologies. Finally, they will have to promote greater competition in the construction and management of infrastructural networks, by means of strategic planning on an international scale.

3. Future scenarios

Any consideration on the future of infrastructural networks must take into account climate change and global warming. Many experts believe that the future will be characterised by increasingly extreme climate events, mainly due to the greenhouse gas emissions of infrastructural systems.

Bearing this situation in mind, it may be useful to try to depict some possible scenarios, suggesting the way in which the infrastructure sector might evolve in the next fifty years. Of course, many uncertainties still exist, such as oil price fluctuations, national energy policies, economic cycles, the pressure of public opinion on environmental issues, conflict-related global instability, etc. The major underlying uncertainty is whether future societies will have the capacity to adopt "intelligent" infrastructural systems engineered for greater efficiency and reduced environmental impact, with all the costs and benefits that this might entail.

For the purpose of outlining possible scenarios, we will draw on a study carried out by the *UK Government's Foresight Programme*[28], a centre of excellence demanded by the UK government (Department for Innovation and Universities) in order to identify potential risks and great opportunities related to scientific progress and new technologies. We will focus our interest on the *Intelligent Infrastructure Systems* study, carried out in 2005 and published the following year, which set out to analyse the possible long-term applications of new technologies to the planning and construction of infrastructural networks. The reference period is until 2050.

The study takes into account around sixty change-inducing factors and predicts four different scenarios: *Perpetual motion, Urban colonies, Tribal trading, Good intentions*.

It is unlikely that the future will bear exact resemblance to any of the following four scenarios, but it will certainly contain some elements of all of them.

Therefore, these scenarios should not be seen as a sort of prophecy. They are meant to enable us to see how the combination of certain events, scientific trends or social transformations can affect the future of our planet.

3.1 Possible scenarios

1) *Perpetual Motion* describes a society where needs and consumption are constantly on the rise. Real time communication and information characterise social interactions and the public is concerned with environmental issues, even though traffic and energy consumption

[28] http://www.foresight.gov.uk/index.html

volumes remain very high, as well as mobility requirements. Air transport is expensive and still uses fossil fuels, even though the use of high-speed trains, hydrogen and other renewables for land transport increase.

A positive economic cycle boosts technological development, which becomes increasingly effective and reliable. The weakness of this scenario lies in the need for conspicuous low-cost energy sources and in the application of new technologies. Although geared towards economic development, new technologies are still too little concerned with environmental sustainability and with the planning of physical environment.

2) In *Urban Colonies*, economic and social policies focus on reducing environmental impact and limiting consumption of non-renewables. People are aware of the damaging effects that unmindful behaviours can have on the environment and endorse conservation-oriented approaches.

People consume less, disposable objects become unpopular, the use of private vehicles is discouraged in favour of "intelligent", "clean", energy-efficient means of public transport, trade is streamlined in order to reduce goods movement, etc. New technologies are conceived to reduce mobility needs and make territories more efficient to ensure environmental sustainability. Rural areas become more isolated and global territorial competitiveness is reduced.

3) *Tribal Trading* describes the world in the aftermath of a dramatic energy crisis. The world has found a new balance, but only after a global recession that has seriously damaged the economic system and

led to a very high unemployment rate. Infrastructural networks are heavily damaged and long-distance journeys have become a luxury that only few people can afford. Similarly, cultural exchanges are limited: for most people the world is reduced to their own local community. Because of the involution of cities, the production of services and foodstuffs is limited to the local scale. The rail network is only used for long-distance journeys with a high added-value. The use of private vehicles is restricted and local transport is normally limited to bicycles and horses.

Competition to secure energy sources has increased and leads to wide scale conflicts. Crime rate is high and unlawfulness widespread. Recycling is not only a good idea: it has become a necessity for economic survival. Technology is limited to the production of equipment that can also function in the event of considerable discontinuity in energy supply. As a consequence, intelligent infrastructural networks are virtually non-existent.

4) *Good Intentions* describes a world where the need to reduce CO_2 emissions refrains individual mobility and, more generally, economic development. Intelligent vehicles provide information on the environmental cost of journeys.

They automatically monitor cruising speed in order to optimise performance and reduce noxious emissions. The distribution of goods is managed through wireless identification technologies that optimise logistics and distribution systems.

Yet in spite of all this, people constantly fear that they are not doing enough to remedy the environmental damages caused by human activities. Society has not yet been able to find truly alternative sources of energy to replace fossil fuels. Reactions to overcome problems are put back in an almost unconscious attempt to preserve current levels of well-being.

Only when environmental problems become an emergency are urgent measures taken, even drastically. Technology has a decisive role in ensuring that harmful emissions are monitored and resources optimised. In the absence of a clean low-cost source of energy, the world is subordinated to the environmental assessment of its own activities. Therefore, planning a functional urban environment capable of reducing mobility requirements and optimising the use of resources acquires an increasingly important role.

After depicting the four scenarios, researchers at the *UK Government's Foresight Programme* used them as case studies and submitted

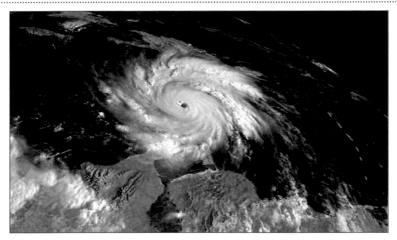

them to the attention of privileged interlocutors: local governors, businesspersons, researchers and students. The methodology used was the full immersion of every single interviewee in each of the four scenarios through a very accurate simulation of their features, perspectives and effects.

Their reactions were then measured using a pre-defined interview model. Reactions were very different. Students clearly expressed their concern about the dangers deriving from an unmindful use of natural resources and stated their willingness to even accept unpopular political choices, provided that they are designed to preserve environmental resources.

On the contrary, other interlocutors, particularly local governors and business persons, were less convinced about it and were more interested in boosting economic development and preserving current levels of well-being.

The interesting part of the study is not really the reactions, which could have been somehow predicted (young generations are more concerned with environmental resources and are willing to pay a price for their conservation).

It is rather the ability to elaborate long-term complex scenarios and compare their degree of acceptance of "intelligent infrastructures", which could play a relevant role in ensuring sustainable development in the future.

3.2 Implications

A widely used definition of "sustainability" is that of a form of development which satisfies current needs without hampering the possibility of future generations to satisfy their own needs. It is commonly agreed that the three sectors on which sustainability can be measured are: 1) environment, 2) society, 3) economy. After elaborating the four scenarios and submitting them to the reactions of selected groups of interlocutors, researchers at the *UK Government's Foresight Programme* tried to understand how in the coming decades the application of scientific and technological innovations to infrastructural networks can contribute to achieving sustainability in the above-mentioned sectors.

Environment[29] - For the next 50 years, the planning and maintenance of infrastructural systems will be most significantly impacted by the effects of climate change and the international policies that will be implemented in order to counter them.

Following current trends, climate change will lead to an average temperature increase of up to 3°C between 2050 and 2080, with summer temperatures exceeding 40°C in today's temperate zones. This will affect all of the four considered scenarios. But what effects can we expect from climate change?

Firstly, floods will become more frequent. This will be due not only to sea level increase as a consequence of glaciers melting, but also to rivers overflowing because of frequent rainfall. Moreover, floods will also come from underground, as water tables will rise and sewerage systems will become overloaded. Increasingly extreme phenomena will bring about more frequent catastrophic weather events, such as tornados or hurricanes, even in areas which are currently not affected by such phenomena. On the other hand, extended periods of drought will become more and more frequent and they could determine water supply insufficiencies. The impact of climate change on infrastructural systems will be very much dependent upon the nature of the infrastructure itself.

During the planning phase, it will be necessary to take into account the most adverse effects of climate change, such as increased land instability due to the alternation of dry spells with periods of violent rainfall. Since floods may become recurrent, they will no longer be considered as extraordinary events and it will be necessary to provide users, for instance, with real-time information systems and alternative routes in the event of inundation.

1

(29) see Osborn D., "Environmental implications", in *Intelligent Infrastructure Futures Scenarios Toward 2055 – Perspective and Process*, UK Office of Science and Technology, London 2006.

Road infrastructures will have to allow for quick and secure communication even under low visibility circumstances (fog, snow, rain) thanks to automated systems for speed and safety distance control and the immediate warning about causes of possible traffic slow-down.

Climate change might also affect the choice of locations suitable for urban settlement. The risk of sea floods, overflowing rivers and overloaded water systems will affect not only the transport system, but might also increase the likelihood of health emergencies, environmental pollution, smog or fog production or even affect the psychophysical balance of people. The quality of life in some urban areas will be at stake.

Furthermore, the possible consequences on public health of a higher hydrogen content in the atmosphere are not yet clearly known, in the event of a shift towards a transport economy based on this propellant.

Society[30] - In the next 50 years, social interactions will be shaped according to the different scenarios.

In the first scenario - *T* - people live in a society that is strongly characterised by networks facilitating long-distance connections and thus favouring both collective and individual mobility.

Frequent journeys are a status symbol of modern life, including those on intercontinental routes. The scope of human activities can no longer be restricted to small territorial contexts, even for the organisation of economic markets which are increasingly geared towards a process of globalisation. This sort of "obsession with the physical presence" cannot be cured even by new teleconference technologies, which can support but cannot replace physical presence in business meetings.

The second scenario - *Urban Colonies* - contains a new urban model of compact cities built with sustainable materials and technologies. The use of private vehicles is discouraged to the advantage of efficient and low-consuming systems of collective transport. The scope of human activities is limited and social interactions take place mainly within the neighbourhood.

Such a scenario could hardly stem from the linear development of existing models or from a pre-defined political strategy. It is more likely to be the result of one or more catastrophic global events that will persuade society to substantially change its life style. A bit like what happened in the Western world, particularly in the US, after the events of 9/11, when freedom restrictions were made acceptable in the name

(30) see Urry J., "Social processes", in *ibid*.

(in that particular case) of national security. The non-sustainability of a consumerist life style could become apparent, for example, after a global dramatic event provoked by climate changes, or by a world war for the ownership of energy resources or for the control over water sources, etc.

The third scenario - *Tribal Trading* - predicts a sort of "New Middle Ages" where society, after a global energy crisis with catastrophic consequences, goes back to a sort of pre-capitalistic condition. In a system of State-Cities fortified by protective barriers and surrounded by a socially dangerous external environment, travel insecurity affects collective mobility and refrains the individual one, making it the privilege of a very rich social class that can afford to use very expensive means of air transport (helicopters, light aircrafts). The control and possession of energy and water resources determine economic empires and large monopolies. Globalised metropolises are difficult to govern.

Thus, many people flee their dangers in order to establish new smaller communities which can be directly governed and which are located in the proximity of energy resources that are essential for their self-sufficiency.

A similar process has somehow already started in many parts of the modern world: the so-called "wild zones", where the role of law and of State authority is limited and the phenomenon of gangs and outlaw violent social communities is rampant. I am referring to some urban areas in the Middle-East, others in the ex Soviet Union, some *favelas* in South America and the poorest areas in Sub-Saharan Africa, but also marginalised neighbourhoods in big European and American metropolises.

The fourth scenario - *Good Intentions* - could be defined of "global sustainability". It stems from the idea that the right to individual mobility should not be necessarily granted if it entails a negative impact on global environmental balances.

This means favouring telepresence through the deployment of ICTs in order to reduce the need for individual mobility in the business sector (videoconference), but also in major everyday life interactions. In this scenario, alternative propellants, such as hydrogen, replace fossil fuels for individual mobility and research for new means of transport is further developed.

Economy[31]- Since the dawn of industrialisation, the economic growth of industrialised countries, measured over a long period of time, has

(31) Köhler Tyndall J., "Economics", in *ibid*.

continued at a rate of about 2% per year. At present, there are three major economic trends on a global scale: 1) globalisation, in other words, the rapid expansion of international exchanges; 2) the structural transformation of advanced economies, which are moving away from the manufacturing sector to the benefit of the service sector; 3) the development of science and technologies, particularly ICTs, which improve the performance of applications while reducing their costs, and at the same time induce changes in social interactions. On the basis of these trends, let us try to evaluate the effects of the afore-mentioned scenarios on global economic structures in the next 50 years.

The first scenario - *Perpetual Motion* - implies a constant economic growth and an intensification of the globalisation process. An increasingly widespread use of ICTs leads to a general transition towards automated services. There is a general tendency towards fiscal federalism, but the administrative authority is still very much centralised and rests on the positive trends of economic growth. Social expenditure is very high as is that of public health services, burdened by the onset of new diseases related to the high level of stress that this model entails.

Private insurance schemes are widely spread. Given the high cost of resources, technological development is used to design particularly efficient production processes capable of minimising energy use while keeping performance at a high level. A new sector of the economy specifically dedicated to these objectives will catch on: "Resource Management".

The second scenario - *Urban Colonies* - contains important changes in the economic structure. This does not necessarily mean that economic growth should come to a standstill. On the contrary, the priorities set out in this scenario aim at preserving very high levels of investment and boosting industrial production. What changes considerably is the consumption model: imported goods are less consumed to the advantage of local production.

The building sector benefits from policies on restructuring. ICTs are constantly growing. The turnover produced by new vehicles designed with environment-friendly technologies has a beneficial effect on the production of vehicles for individual mobility. Recycling and resource management are consolidated and become indispensable for production. Fiscal policies and key public services (school, health) are decentralised at local government level and this contributes to increasing the divide between urban and rural areas, which are doomed to decline and depopulation.

The third scenario - *Tribal Trading* - stems from a very serious energy crisis. The economic depression sparked by very high prices of energy sources has completely wiped out national economies. The international financial system has disappeared and has been replaced by local bilateral agreements that resort, among other things, to forms of barter.

Consumption is almost exclusively directed towards local production. Military expenditure, which is required to ensure the protection of local communities, absorbs a considerable percentage of their budgets. Industrial cycles are deeply affected by recycling needs and by the absence of sophisticated logistic systems.

The fourth scenario - *Good Intentions* - contains some of the economic elements analysed in the first scenario. The major difference is the

limitation of individual mobility and the reduction of long-distance connections, which will have repercussions on various productive sectors, such as tourism.

The limitation of overall mobility affects the localisation of production activities, which will be more and more subordinated to transport and energy supply costs.

From the description of the four scenarios and the analysis of their implications, a common element emerges: in all of them, digital networks and scientific research are indispensable to optimise the performance of production processes and make them "intelligent", i.e. capable of reacting to external inputs.

3.3 Intelligent infrastructures

An "intelligent" infrastructural system is one which has been planned, constructed and managed using appropriate information and communication technologies in order to obtain the highest level of efficiency: higher performance with lower resource consumption. The issues of global climate change and energy saving have to be at the heart of any possible discussion on the future of infrastructural networks.

There are at least four ways in which intelligence can be applied to infrastructural networks:

1) planning infrastructures in an intelligent way;
2) obtaining intelligent information from infrastructures;
3) planning intelligent applications that will be integrated in the infrastructures;
4) using infrastructures in an intelligent way.

From a physical point of view, an *Intelligent Infrastructure System* is not so different from current infrastructures. The differences lie in the way in which the system reacts to external inputs and in the services that it can provide to its users. Road infrastructures, for example, can provide information to the drivers using them, thus enabling them to modify their road map. The application of artificial intelligence will make it possible to reduce the driver's mental effort, by allowing him to entrust many of the vehicle control tasks to the automatic systems. The result is a safer, more efficient and less energy-consuming transport system capable of managing grater traffic volumes without creating congestion.

An intelligent infrastructure that provides detailed information on the cost of a trip (in economic, social and environmental terms) could even persuade us to reduce the total volume of journeys, avoiding those which can be replaced by other forms of communication. It is therefore plausible that people will continue to travel, but they will change the purpose of their journeys. There will be an increasing tendency to concentrate business, leisure and residence in the same place. Moreover, the development of ICTs will increase the possibility to work at home and thus have a positive impact on commuting phenomena.

In general, people are rather reluctant to pay in order to get real-time information on the trip that they are making. It is therefore difficult to conceive a commercial business for this type of services. However, should it be proved that drivers change their habits thanks to a suitable information system, for example by reducing the volume of journeys if they are aware of their overall costs, then government

authorities could take measures to support the provision of accurate travel information services for the benefit of the entire community. Traffic jams or even traffic slowing down could be averted if drivers received immediate information on traffic conditions. At present, all the information that one can receive while driving consists in radio messages broadcast by specialised stations (in Italy for example, we have "Isoradio FM 103.3") and, sometimes, the electronic variable message panels that can mostly be found along motorways. Technology can do much more! Using satellite navigation possibilities, we can gather real-time information on traffic, elaborate it and give it back to drivers in a targeted way (i.e. in a detailed and personalised way, according to the geographic area of interest) though their GPS, palmtops or mobile phones. According to traffic conditions, it is also possible to suggest alternative routes that can be displayed on the mobile peripheral device, with an indication of the travel time.

In order to optimise the use of infrastructures, traffic volumes can be reduced by improving the efficiency of journey planning, especially for freight transport. The telematic management of markets and the attentive analysis of the origin and destination of goods should provide the basis for reducing travel time of transport lorries: a commonly mentioned example is that of mineral water (with its pros and cons). Despite the existence of a multitude of trademarks scattered

all over Italy, they all have a virtually identical content of sodium and other mineral salts. And yet, lorries full of mineral waters produced in the south of Italy jam up motorways to reach northern markets and vice versa[32].

The planning of intelligent infrastructures requires at least three simultaneous actions.

Firstly, we need an adequate urban planning scheme capable of creating synergies between infrastructural policies and other territorial strategies: such as identification of residential areas, environmental sustainability, landscape values, etc.

Secondly, it is important that production is as local as possible, in accordance with market rules. Over the past 50 years, we have witnessed considerable changes in production cycles and in the distribution of production sites. Most of the goods consumed in industrialised countries are produced abroad, often in another continent. Globalisation has detached markets from production sites and has determined an exponential increase in goods transport. We are used to thinking that the products we use are entirely manufactured within an industrial plant. It is no longer the case! For some time now, most of the industrial products that we consume have undergone a process of "deverticalisation". Every single phase of the production process is performed in a different plant; each plant is located in a different

(32) I do not intend to trivialise such a complex and sensitive mechanism as the economic market, with all its different facets that depend on situations of monopoly or oligopoly, competition, variable, fixed and transition costs, etc. I simply want to stress that the use of infrastructures is on the brink of collapse, because, among other things, of an excessive transport of goods by road, thus determining an environmental impact for the community that is hardly sustainable in the long term.

area of the continent or even the globe, where specialisation in that particular production phase is higher and labour costs are lower. It is therefore possible that the fabric of the jeans we are wearing is manufactured in China, cut in Tunisia, sawn in Turkey and labelled in Italy. Just like production models, selling patterns are also subject to change. Over the past 50 years, we have seen a move away from central distribution outlets in favour of large hypermarkets in peripheral areas. In the next 50 years, we will see an increase in on-line sales, which will have an impact on warehousing, goods distribution systems and transport models. Enterprises will try to develop increasingly flexible products, in order to create economies of scale and satisfy the increasing demand for product personalisation, which will become a fundamental added-value to counter economies' migration towards low-cost production areas. The whirling global movement of goods will be slowed down due to the deverticalisation process. On the one hand, labour costs in developing countries will increase as union representation develops there, and on the other hand, higher costs of fossil fuels and the difficulties in procuring alternative sources will make energy an increasingly precious good, making people less inclined to waste it. This will lead to transport costs having a considerable impact on production processes and, therefore, to the possible reduction of excesses in the deverticalisation process.

Thirdly, the construction of intelligent infrastructures could be supported by integrated intermodal transport systems: vehicles moving along the infrastructure could be part of it rather than belonging to private owners. A centralised system could monitor overall mobility (by road, rail and air) and dynamically respond to the needs of each user. Vehicles could behave as a sort of remotely controlled "swarm" in order to achieve the highest level of service efficiency. In so doing, it should also be possible to maximise the yield of the fleet, for example, by avoiding that a vehicle remains unused for a long time or by organising a central recycling service for all materials. An artificial intelligence could be applied to vehicles and could be in charge of most driving responsibilities. Some modern vehicles already have visual and acoustic sensors that function as parking aids. We should simply apply the same principle to gearing functions. We could even create trains of vehicles that drive together along the same road and follow the same itinerary at the same speed, which is checked by an electronic stripe along the carriageway. Furthermore, this system makes it possible for disabled and elderly people to travel under adverse weather conditions (fog, heavy rainfall), thus putting an end to driving restrictions on age grounds. But the greatest benefit of all would be the drastic reduction of road accident causes and, therefore, of casualties. In such a system, the energy required to activate the vehicle fleet could conceivably be produced by the infrastructure itself, using innovative environment-friendly technologies that benefit from the linear development of the infrastructure.

Based on these suggestions, we can try to draw a summary of the planning actions that could contribute to the achievement of Intelligent Infrastructure Systems, as they have been described so far.

INTELLIGENT INFRASTRUCTURES

PLANNING ACTIONS	QUALITY CRITERIA
1. Obtaining intelligent information from infrastructures	
1.1 Parking	Digital systems provide information on the availability of parking space in the city centre. Digital controllers monitor the saturation of public parking space and send information on the availability of space and suggestions on how to get there directly to the mobile devices available in the vehicle (GPS, smart phones, palmtops).
1.2 Traffic	Systems of sensors and cameras installed in crucial points of the infrastructure elaborate data on traffic and traffic jams. Besides communicating with variable message panels along the infrastructure, the systems send information to the mobile devices available in the car (GPS, smart phones, palmtops) suggesting alternative routes and travel time.
1.3 Monitoring	Monitoring systems capable of signalling malfunctions in the various components of the infrastructure and of the technologies that are applied to it: digital devices and connected sensors, security devices, driving tutoring, conditions of road surface, obstacles in the carriageway, etc. An operating rapid intervention centre elaborates the information.
2. Planning intelligent applications that will be integrated in infrastructures	
2.1 Solar Energy	Systems of solar panels are located along the infrastructural network, next to the crash barrier on the internal side of the lane. The system produces energy which is stored and then distributed to electric vehicles in special service/parking areas. In so doing, the infrastructure operator is also an electrical energy producer and operator at the same time.
2.2 Drive Sensors	A system of sensors and detection stations is located along the infrastructure and communicates with similar devices available in the car. The system is capable of providing information to an artificial intelligence on board of the infrastructure car fleet, which allows for its control: speed, itinerary, safety distance, driving control, reaction to causes of accidents, etc.
2.3 Smart Car	The infrastructure car fleet is endowed with an artificial intelligence capable of communicating with the infrastructure and putting it in charge of part or all of the driving responsibilities. Private cars are also endowed with similar devices and can choose different degrees of driving automation, according to their specific needs and itineraries.

PLANNING ACTIONS	QUALITY CRITERIA
3. Using infrastructures in an intelligent way	
3.1 Integrated system	Integrated intermodal transport systems. Vehicles moving along the infrastructure are part of it and do not belong to private owners. The vehicle fleet runs on electricity and is refuelled with energy produced by the infrastructure itself. A centralised mobility monitoring system responds dynamically to the needs of every user by interacting with the vehicle.
3.2 Remote control	Vehicles behave as a sort of remotely controlled "swarm". Rows of vehicles move together along sections of the infrastructure following itineraries and speeds which are managed by a centralised digital system. Security in adverse weather conditions (fog, heavy rainfall) is higher, just like drivability for disabled and elderly people. Reduced risk of fatal accidents.
3.3 Rolling stock	The infrastructure car fleet optimises car use and maintenance operations, prevents vehicles from remaining unused for a long time, exploits economies of scale in purchasing processes, organises a centralised service for the recycling of all materials, provides cars with the necessary digital devices to enable them to communicate with the centralised monitoring system.
4. Engineering cars in an intelligent way	
4.1 Project	Sustainable urban planning creates synergies between infrastructural policies and other territorial strategies in order to distribute functions adequately on the territory. Executive infrastructural planning with the introduction of digital panels, sensors, pollutants detection stations, photovoltaic panels, etc.
4.2 Environment	Mitigated impact of infrastructural works and proper integration in the territorial context. Sustainability should not be restricted to landscape and environmental aspects, but should also concern society (NIMBY phenomena), economy (works financing), energy consumption and polluting emissions (CO_2, noise, dusts, etc.)
4.3 Digital road	According to the time slot and the traffic conditions detected by the digital monitoring system, sections of the infrastructure connected to the city can increase the number of lanes giving access to or departing from the city centre, change one-way signs, close/open road segments. An automated coordination centre elaborates the data and adopts decisions in order the smooth urban mobility.

1. Solar panels along infrastructures
2. Filling station powered by solar energy
3. Toyota i-Unit, prototype of an ultra-compact electrical vehicle

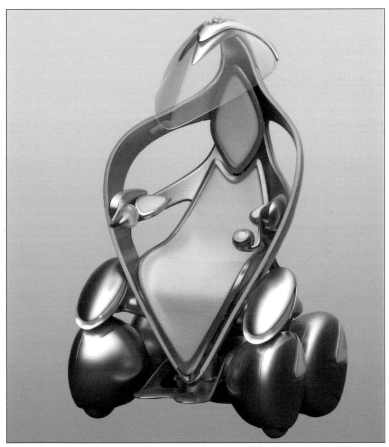

4. Toyota i-Unit in upright position

4. Digital networks

We will now dwell upon a particular category of infrastructural networks, the digital networks, describing their evolution and reflecting upon the impact they are having on modern society and territories.

4.1 The dawn of networks[33].

The year 1969 will always be remembered in human history as the year when the first man landed on the moon. However, there is at least another reason why this should be considered the beginning of a new era: the appearance of internet.

Actually, internet and the conquest of space are closely linked. In 1957 the Soviet Union achieved a very important space mission: the *Sputnik*[34] was put into orbit. This event had huge repercussions both on the national pride of United States of America and on their security measures in the military field. The American reaction arrived shortly afterwards: towards the end of the 50s, in the middle of the Cold War, the Eisenhower administration allocated considerable funds to military research in the communication sector. Following approval in the Congress, in 1958 the US Defence Department created *ARPA* (*Advanced Research Projects Agency*), whose headquarters were established in the Pentagon, Washington.

Meanwhile, the Soviet space successes continued and in 1961 Yuri Gagarin was the first man to complete an entire elliptic orbit around the Earth, reaching a maximum distance of 300 km and travelling at a speed of 27.000 km/hour. The remarkable worldwide coverage of the event led the US to make even greater efforts in the field of aerospace research. In 1958, the government had already created NASA (*National Aeronautics and Space Administration*) entrusted with the specific task of managing space programmes. Consequently, ARPA had to focus increasingly on its statutory research objectives, thus moving away from the aerospace field. Given the availability of expensive electronic labs, it decided to develop a project that could enable those machines to communicate with each other and transfer data to a net of computers located in different areas.

The Arpanet network was thus created in 1969. From the very beginning, it involved four important American research centres: UCLA (University of Los Angeles), UCSB (University of Santa Barbara), the University of Utah and SRI (Stanford Research Institute). The development of Arpanet was progressive. In 1971, the network consisted of 15 nodes and 23 hosts connected to each other, including the NASA computers. There were a few hundred users. The interface and data transfer software followed the so-called FTP protocol (File Transfer

(33)In this paragraph, I use a lot of information tapped from: Bonacina D. "Internet dalle origini al terzo millennio", (*Internet from its origins to the third millennium*), working paper published on http://bonacina.wordpress.com

(34) The Sputnik programme consists of a series of space missions - not involving human beings - which were promoted by the Soviet Union at the end of the 50s and which aimed at testing the use of artificial satellites. All the Sputniks were put into orbit by the R-7 carrier rocket, engineered for military purposes.

1. Wernher von Braun and John F. Kennedy

Protocol), which is still used nowadays. Over time, they underwent considerable changes, establishing new specific communication techniques which, as a whole, were identified as TCP (Transmission Control Protocol). In 1978, the protocol was further developed and was divided in two parts: the TCP for the management of data packages and the IP (Internet Protocol) to channel them. Since then, the couple TCP/IP has represented the base of modern internet conception: today every computer connected to the internet has its own IP address. Towards the end of the 70s, Arpanet was still made up of only 15 knots connecting university research centres, but hundreds of IT departments in the US were also developing similar needs. In order to prevent them from being excluded from communication developments, the National Science Foundation (NSF) began to finance the set-up of cheaper networks between various university centres, connected through the TCP/IP protocol.

Soon, an increasingly wide system of networks started to develop around *Arpanet*, while research developments started to focus on another important aspect: data transmission rates. The Universities

1. First rocket launches from Cape Canaveral, during the 50s
2. Landing on the Moon, 1969
3. Yuri Gagarin

of Princeton and Pittsburgh, together with other research centres, had particularly advanced elaborators and the NSF decided to invest in the set-up of a network that could connect them with a 56k line (the rate of current – obsolete – analogical modems). The success of the connection spurred all American universities to uphold the proposal of the *NSF* and create the *NSFnet*. The number of users climbed to ten thousand. In 1988, *NSFnet* had to increase the line speed to 1.5 Mbps in order to make it suitable for the increasing number of connected terminals. The same year, *IRC* (Internet Replay Chat) was created, the first chat that allowed all users to communicate in writing in real time. One year later, the number of users increased tenfold. The "old" *Arpanet* had already marked time and could no longer compete with *NSFnet*. In 1989, *Arpanet* officially ceased to exist and all its nodes were transferred to the new network.

At the beginning of the 90s, *NSFnet* access policy was changed to allow for the entry of non-scientific information, such as corporate or market information. This marked the beginning of an expansion process which soon became inexorable. The number of users was almost uncontrollable, just like the data packages being transferred. Shortly afterwards, the necessity arose to conceive network safety measures: in 1988, the first virus was already detected, damaging more than 60,000 connected computers. The European contribution to the structure of the net started in the first half of the 90s: researchers from the *European Organization for Nuclear Research* (CERN) in Geneva developed a system which allowed to consult information, data and images in an intuitive way and which later developed into the *World Wide Web* (www). The Web, the modern internet configuration, was finally created. Consultation was made smooth thanks to the *Hyper Text Markup Language* (HTML), the language which started to be used for the creation of most websites. Soon, the first browsers were conceived: the first was probably *Mosaic* (1993) of the *National Center for Supercomputing Applications*, followed by *Netscape Navigator* (1994) and *Microsoft Internet Explorer* (1995).

4.2 New economy[35]

Internet development laid the foundations for a phenomenon which would characterise future years, with all its positive and negative consequences: the *New Economy*. This term (together with all the parallel definitions it has acquired over time, such as net-economy, e-economy, knowledge-based economy, i-economy, etc.) was coined towards the end of the 90s to describe the evolution from an economy based on

(35) In this paragraph I use a lot of information tapped from: Maurizio Zenezini "È finita la New economy?", (*Is the New economy over?*), working paper n. 89 published by the Department of Economics and Statistics of the University of Trieste http://www.univ.trieste.it/~nirdses

manufacturing and industrial production to an economy essentially based on services and managed through digital networks, particularly the internet.

The new economy is not really an economy of enterprises that use the internet, but rather a business model where IT networks become essential for organisational and operating purposes. Just like the old industrial economy was not that of electricity producing companies, but rather the economy of enterprises that functioned thanks to electricity[36]. It is especially in the US that, during the 90s, the rate of productivity skyrocketed thanks to the deployment of new information and communication technologies. The booming value of technological securities (NASDAQ index) in the New York Stock Exchange became an accurate indicator for the new economic model. If we add to that the fact that, during the same years, European economies were striving to comply with the Maastricht parameters, we can easily understand why the international debate on "information society"[37] engaged researchers, politicians and economists for such a long time.

A rhetorical discourse, fuelled by the media, started to develop around the New Economy and made the debate quickly slide into ideological simplification. Thus, Nicholas Negroponte, as director of the M.I.T. MediaLab, stated that *digital technology is a natural force that will bring increased universal harmony to everyone in the world*[38]. But Al Gore, recent Nobel Peace Prize winner and ex vice-president of the US, went even further and described his "IT Motorways" programme as *the vehicle for a new Athenian area of global democracy*[39].

As Duguid[40] wrote quite polemically, this euphoria for the New Economy led to a true wave of "endisms". It was said that, with the New Economy, television, press and means of communication would come to an end, just like brokers, businesses and bureaucracy, schools and universities. Politics, governments and national States would also come to an end. IT technologies would revolutionise social, economic and political relationships. It was said… Then, almost unexpectedly, the stock exchange bubble of the New Economy burst, as we all know. And after the amazing tumble of shares and the consequent bankruptcy of many enterprises, many people anticipated the death of internet and quite often these were the same people who, a couple of years before, had praised it so highly and described it as a panacea for the development of all mankind.

Quite simply, it is more likely that internet is neither dead nor is it a miracle. On the contrary, as some researchers[41] have pointed out,

(36) see Castells M., "La città delle reti", cit. (*The city of networks*)
(37) see Mattelart A., "Histoire de la société de l'information", 2001; trad. En. *History of the information society*, Einaudi, Turin 2002.
(38) see Stoll C., "High-Tech Heretic", 1999; It. Ed., Garzanti, Milan 2001.
(39) see Mattelart A., op. cit.
(40) see Duguid P., "The Social Life of Information", Harvard Business School Press, Harvard, Mass.
(41) see De Biase L., Meletti G. (edited by), "Bidone.com?", Fazi Editore, Milan 2001.

1. Bill Gates

the bursting of the stock exchange bubble was actually beneficial because it got rid of those who had seen the internet as a sheer instrument to make quick money, while maintaining the promise of a more concrete internet, which is not an end in itself but rather a means to reduce communication costs and time. Clearly, there was an excess of initial optimism vis-à-vis the commercial potential of internet, which induced a tremendous amount of unwise investments. Nevertheless, the fundamental changes introduced by the wave of new IT technologies persist, internet commercial applications have started to become important, although not at the "supersonic" pace predicted a few years ago. The scope of business network activities is increasing, just like digital applications in logistics management. Home banking is spreading increasingly fast, enabling users to perform all bank and financial operations from their homes and leaving behind the memories of never-ending queues at the front office. In some commercial sectors, e-commerce has turned websites into true "virtual windows", has increased the possibility for buyers to select their products and, above all, has eliminated the need for warehousing, with considerable savings for the seller. Tour operators' travel packages can only be consulted and purchased on-line, either by the client sitting comfortably at home or by the delegated travel agency. In other words, the revolution has taken place. Oh yes, it has!

4.3 Broadband

In common language the term "broadband" is used to indicate telecommunication systems that allow for internet access at high data transmission rates[42]. It is a fact that IT applications and network services evolve in a way that requires increasingly high bandwidth. If today a few hundred Kb/s for private use can still be considered sufficient, in the sort/middle term it will be necessary to have a bandwidth of a few Mb/s. Today businesses and public administrations work with bandwidths of a few Mb/s, but in the future they will have to adopt much higher band capacities. The current scenario in terms of internet access technologies is complex and diversified. There are telecommunication systems allowing for cable internet connections, using the copper telephone line or optic fibre cables or using the copper network for electric supply (Powerline). There are also telecommunication systems allowing for wireless internet connections using radio frequencies, such as WiFi and WiMax, satellite connections, third generation UMTS telephony or digital television. For private use (families, small businesses) there are currently no alternatives capable of competing - from an economic, technical or distribution point of view - with access through telephone networks. However, it is likely that in the middle to long term more evolved and performing transmission technologies might take root, such as optic fibre, bidirectional satellite or WiMax networks.

The applications conveyed through these broadband systems will have a heavy impact on end-users, citizens and public administrations. One of these applications is the so-called "virtual presence", particularly resulting in teleconference, distance-learning, telemedicine, teleworking and remote-supervision systems. The importance of these applications lies in their ability to bring about considerable changes in the relationships between the people involved, thus generating innovative interaction mechanisms compared to the traditional ones. Another application is the so-called *Peer to Peer*, which consists in the creation of on-line communities of users who mutually exchange services and information, through a centralised coordination system. It is the system preferred by young people to exchange music files, videos or software. ASP services (*Application Service Providing*) can also be developed thanks to broadband networks. In this particular case, IT tools, both hardware and software, together with the professional skills required for their management, are not necessarily found in the user's location but can be found in the location of the service provider.

(42) Lately, recommendation I.113 of the Standardization Sector of the ITU (International Telecommunication Union) defined broadband as a transmission capacity that is faster than primary rate ISDN, at 1.5 (in the USA) or 2.0 Mb/s in Europe. However, transmission speeds that are equal to 256 kb/s are commonly sold as "broadband", at least by service providers. It is useful to remind ourselves that traditional analogical modems allow for maximum transmission speeds of 56 kb/s in download, whilst ISDN connections go as far as 128 kb/s.

ASP provision modalities are particularly interesting for small and medium enterprises, which can thus resort to high quality services without having to equip themselves directly with expensive tools and skills for functions that do not represent their core business.
Examples of other relevant services delivered through broadband networks can be found in the field of e-government. They aim at improving the relationship between citizens and public administrations through improved data accessibility and greater procedural transparency. As for telemedicine services and applications, the core element is also the

(43) see "La larga banda in Italia", publication by the Ugo Bordoni Foundation presented at the Informal Council of the EU Telecommunication Ministers which took place in Viterbo from the 4th to the 5th September 2003.
(44) The ADSL technology (*Asymmetric Digital Subscriber Line*), which belongs to the family of DSL technologies, allows for high speed internet access (more than 640 kb/s). With ADSL, transmission speed is asymmetric: data transmission speed to the subscriber is higher than data transmission from the subscriber, in order to optimise the quantity of available band, ta-

use of IP protocol networks and the availability of high transmission bandwidth throughout the territory.

For telemedicine, we encompass the whole of the IT and medical techniques allowing for remote treatment of patients or, more generally, for remote provision of health services. In the field of clinical diagnosis, a doctor can perform a diagnosis on a patient who is not physically in the same room, through the remote transmission of data gathered by diagnosis instruments. The medical *second opinion* is one of the most common applications in the field of tele-medicine. It consists in remotely providing a clinical opinion supported by data which are gathered and sent to a remote doctor who analyses and uses the data for a medical report, thus producing a second clinical evaluation of the patient. This can even be used in the event of particularly complex surgical interventions. Reforming the public health sector requires, among other things, the concentration of hospital centres of excellence and the downgrading of peripheral units. These units could find a new role thanks to telemedicine and be used for remote treatment of patients or, more generally, for remote provision of on-line health services.

The list of applications that could be developed thanks to broadband telecommunication systems could be very long. However, the aforementioned examples are enough to show that it is probably impossible to identify one single application that could alone justify the need for an extensively widespread network infrastructure throughout the territory or that could indeed determine its success or spontaneous deployment. It is more appropriate to talk about a set of applications which, individually or collectively, can only spread through residential and professional areas in the presence of a widespread broadband infrastructure.[43].

In Italy, the pace of broadband deployment is a success story. The increase in access points has been the result of concomitant factors which have positively interacted with each other. On the one hand, telecommunication operators and *Internet Service Providers* have developed an increasingly wide and innovative offer, in terms of performance but also in terms of contents and tariff plans. On the other hand, the expansion of ADSL[44] coverage, from 40% of the population in 2001 to about 88% in September 2006, has created the makings for the full unfolding of market forces' beneficial effects[45]. Nonetheless, the infrastructural digital divide[46] continues to exist and affects most regions, regardless of their economic potential. More specifi-

king into account the fact that normally private users require more incoming information than outgoing information.

(45) Source: *BroadBand Observatory – Between* (2006)

(46) Digital divide refers to the gap existing between those who can access new technologies (internet, personal computers) available worldwide and those who, on the contrary, cannot do it for different reasons, such as low income, ignorance or lack of infrastructures (here we can specifically talk about infrastructural digital divide).

cally, areas with the highest level of ADSL coverage are metropolitan areas and territorial zones that are easier to "infrastructurise" due to their morphology (plains and densely populated areas). Apulia, Lombardy, Lazio and Liguria have the highest levels of ADSL coverage, exceeding 90% of the population. At the bottom of the scale, we have Molise, Aosta Valley and Basilicata, where more than one inhabitant in four is not reached by ADSL coverage. In September 2006, 12% of the Italian population (around 6 million people) was living in infrastructure *digital divide areas*, i.e. areas where broadband connectivity is solely possible through expensive ad-hoc connections or through satellite solutions, rather than through the current reference technology for broadband: ADSL.

Clearly, the digital divide phenomenon goes well beyond simple geographical differences between broadband served areas and those which are not, involving cultural, social, economic, civil and other differences. Nonetheless, it is true that to ensure a uniform territorial spread of internet use advantages (to citizens, enterprises, governments), an insufficient but necessary condition is the overcoming of difficulties related to the setting-up of broadband infrastructures in areas where operators deem it unprofitable to carry out infrastructural investments.

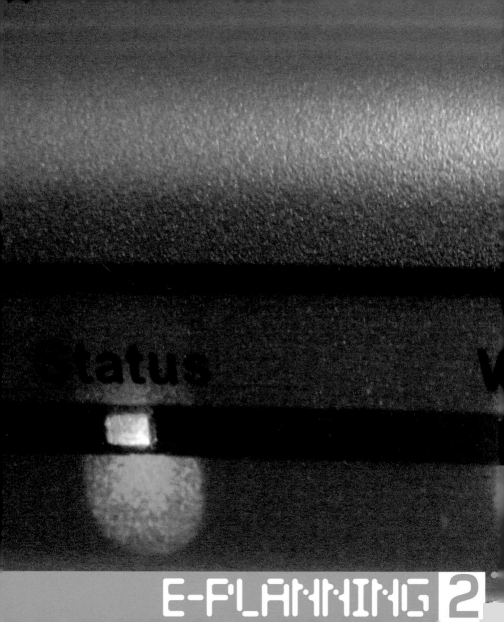

5. Digital networks and territorial governance

Let us now focus our attention on the innovations that new information technologies, particularly internet, are prompting in urban science and in territorial and urban transformation processes. Let us begin by observing the way in which the use of internet is contributing to innovating university research and methodologies. Then, we will dwell upon the use of internet in the urban profession and in public administrations with competencies in the field of territorial governance.

5.1 E-jobs

The computer, even before internet, brought about the true revolution in the urban profession and, more generally, in the architect profession. Not long ago, project blueprints or urban analyses were still handmade, thanks to the painstaking work of the most skilful collaborators. The "amanuensis" skills of a few, so much appreciated since time immemorial, were suddenly overwhelmed by a different kind of ability which is maybe less artistic, but certainly not less creative and, above all, within the grasp of many, particularly young people: *Computer Aided Design* (CAD) and software for architectural and urban sciences. Within a very short time, a very precious object, the very symbol of the architect profession – the drafting machine – disappeared from professional offices and was replaced by the computer. The wonderful Zucor that parents, not without sacrifice, would buy for their son in the first year of architectural studies and which would beautifully stand out in rooms that were always too small to host it, has been replaced by very powerful notebooks with 17'' screens and wireless connections. A true revolution! Not only of the technological planning tool, but also of the very approach to the project itself.

In the beginning, IT technologies were used in a hybrid way. The designer would sketch a handmade draft, then the young CAD expert (or GIS for urban planning bureaus) would translate the project into a digital form. But shortly afterwards, the whole planning was entirely computerised, which made it possible to explore innovative paths of digital architecture. But even "traditional" architecture can use the computer as a tool to carry forward innovation and field research: I wonder whether many of the projects of the most famous deconstructionists (Gehry for example) would have been possible without the computer...

In urban planning, the calculating capacity of computers and of increasingly specific software allow for operations which would have required considerable efforts beforehand. If we take the difficult method of cartographic triangulation to measure the allocation of standards for a General Town Planning Scheme and compare it with the simple cal-

culations automatically generated by current software, we cannot help smiling. And this is just one of the many simplifications that computers have introduced in our daily work. More specifically, as regards the use of internet in professional sectors, besides the importance of e-mails and the possibility to search databases or institutional websites, we should underline the usefulness of public administration portals, which are generally rich in information and offer a wide range of multimedia possibilities.

Up to a few years ago, for example, in order to be informed about public calls, tenders and competitions, one needed to subscribe to the Official Journal and spend a lot of time looking for the required piece of information. Today, there are specific portals providing daily updated information on the wide spectrum of public competitions and tenders, with the possibility to download all the informative material. If we analyse the web portal of any provincial capital, we realise that it offers a wide range of services to architects or urban experts. Portals are organised by thematic sections, which are specific to each municipality, but generally contain information on institutional bodies, municipal enterprises, the registry office, constituencies, sport and tourist activities, mobility, transports, social activities, public services, etc. The most relevant sections for the architect are those related to environment, statistical analyses, registry office services, in addition, of course, to specific environmental fields, urban planning and public works. These sections contain a great deal of information ranging from simple addresses, offices opening hours and administrative procedures (with the possibility to download forms and copies) to official downloadable documents, such as the tables and standards of a General Town Planning Scheme. As a general rule, in order to carry out this operation, the portal requires the user to register him/herself by entering his/her personal data or sometimes requires the possession of an electronic ID card.

After these very simple steps, the user has the possibility to consult the General Town Planning Scheme and print its tables. A useful service, if we think that before we had to go personally to the municipal offices!

However, the true qualitative leap forward for public administration web portals is possible when the authority is equipped with a Territorial Information System.

5.2 Geographic Information System[47]

Out of all the different products introduced by the IT revolution over the past few years, the *Geographic Information System* (GIS), also called Territorial Informative System (TIS), represents an important innovation for the management of data with a geographic component.

These systems are based on the combination of two core elements of IT innovation: computerised design (CAD) and relational databases (DBMS).

The former allows for computerised design of geographical entities, the latter allows for storage of data and information related to these entities.

The combination of these two systems in the GIS has made it possible to overcome the compromise which is inherent to any cartographic representation: any representation of geographical entities is always somehow symbolic and in scale, i.e. it is based on representation criteria whereby a given symbol on the map (ex. a small square) represents a real object with specific geometrical properties (ex. a house)

Although, after centuries of experience, cartographers have developed very fine and consolidated representation techniques (an illustrative example is the legend of a topographic map of the Military Geographical Institute), the symbolic representation of a traditional geographical or thematic map impedes the full understanding of all the information. For instance, even though it is quite simple to symbolically represent the outline of a building, it is not as easy or convenient to symbolically represent the number of floors of the same building, the surface area of individual apartments, the list of tenants living there, the presence of garages or cellars underground, etc.

This limit has been overcome thanks to the spread of the GIS, which makes it possible to analyse a geographical entity both from a geometrical and symbolic perspective and from an informational point of view. In practical terms, these systems create a link between each geographical entity of a map and a database, through the software engineering capabilities.

Territorial Information Systems are specifically created to organise those data, which otherwise would remain scattered among different offices and bodies, and make them accessible to citizens.

TISs are more than just an on-line repository of territorial data which, despite their being efficiently updated and organised, still suffer from the inherent inertia of information archives posted on the web.

TISs are more like a daily working tool for public administration, citi-

[47] see CGT on-line Centre of Geotechnologies of the University of Siena, "Cosa sono i Sistemi Informativi Geografici", *(What are Geographical Information Systems?*), published on http:// geotecnologie.unisi.it

1. and 2. Images taken from the display screen of the "ArcView" Geographic Information System

zens, authorities and businesses, concentrating data management and data consultation and distribution in the same environment.

TISs are at the same time an information tool for citizens and a shared workspace for public administration, where the various offices can consult, add or edit data. Of course, everything will depend on the commitment and willingness of public administration to use the full potential of the TIS, by not confining them to a purely technological sphere, but using them to improve their relationship with citizens through political choices that increase information transparency and accessibility.

There are several types of TIS which differ either in their software platforms or in their content consultation modalities. Perhaps, it is too early to talk about consolidated TIS models.

Nonetheless, following the experiences implemented by different municipalities - which are no longer sporadic – it is possible to identify a set of minimal information contents, which can be seen as "indispensable" and refer to the following thematic sections: basic cartography, land register, general town planning scheme, buildings registry, street guide and public services. As a consequence, citizens and professionals operating within but also outside local administrations and working on the territory on a daily basis can have access to a great deal of information and technical materials (cartographies, cadastral maps, sections of the general town planning scheme, technological networks, etc.) directly on their computer thanks to a simple internet connection.

This is not just about providing databases but also about creating new instruments to manage territorial governance processes which can affect the way in which these very instruments are elaborated.

5.3 E-government

In Italy, the first regional regulatory interventions on IT systems took place towards the end of the 70s. However, it is during the 90s that various projects for the construction of the so-called RUPAR (Regional United Networks of Public Administration) were initiated. They were created by extending telematic connections from regional administrations' headquarters towards health services (Usl-Asl) and towards provinces, municipalities, mountain communities, etc. However, these networks were essentially used for the internal management of administrative processes and mostly involved technicians from public administrations.

With the spread of internet over the past decade, public administrations have started to use the net to try to improve their relationship with citizens, by setting out to increase interaction with offices, improve data accessibility and, above all, increase procedural transparency. In other words, they have placed greater focus on political aspects than on technical ones.

Internet is therefore more than just a new technological tool facilitating access to information. It can also contribute to redefining tasks and procedures of various public offices, through a set of different initiatives which fall under the definition of *e-government*. In an attempt to define this concept, we could say that *e-government* is the process of computerisation of public administration which, in conjunction with an internal procedural reorganisation, allows for the processing of documents through the use of *Information and Communication Technology* (ICT). This is all meant to speed up the work of public authorities and offer users (citizens and enterprises) faster and innovative services. Through the e-Europe[48] programme and the Structural Funds[49], which have encouraged and oriented member States policies in this field, the European Union has given important impetus to e-government. In Italy, we can identify two phases in the implementation of *e-government*[50].

The first phase took place between 2001 and 2003, through targeted State financing (around 300 million Euros) intended to support projects for the development of infrastructural services and user services. These projects aimed, on the one hand, at increasing public administration efficiency and, on the other had, at improving coherence and integration between the local level and the national system. In spring 2003, all the conventions for the initiation of projects were signed. Then, between June 2003 and March 2004, the executive planning of

(48) e-Europe is a programme establishing rules for the liberalisation of telecommunications and the setting-up of a legal framework of reference for e-trade and for the support to industries and the research sector. For further details on the programme, visit: http://europa.eu.int/information _ society/eeurope/2005/index _ en.htm
(49) The Structural Funds and the Cohesion Fund are the financial instruments of the EU regional policy. Their aim is to equalise the level of development among regions and member States.
(50) see Subioli P., "Il ruolo della comunicazione nell'e-government" (*The role of communication in e-government*) on the on-line magazine *Cronache dell'e-government* (*Facts about E-government*) http://www.cronache-egovernment.it/

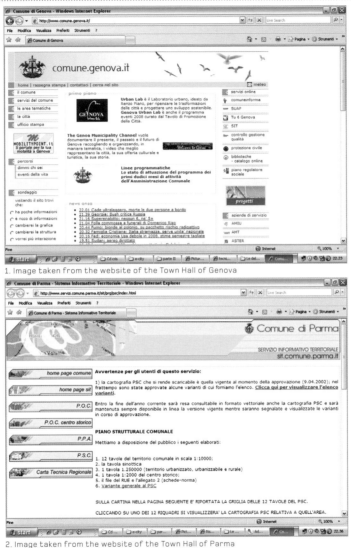

1. Image taken from the website of the Town Hall of Genova

2. Image taken from the website of the Town Hall of Parma

co-financed projects was carried out as a preliminary step for the monitoring of work progress.

The main goal of the second phase of e-government implementation (with funds for about 200 million Euros) was to extend the previously launched innovation processes to most local administrations, by implementing both infrastructural services and services for citizens and businesses. The objective by 2005 was to achieve the maximum level of territorial and demographic coverage through the on-line provision of a specific list of 80 priority services for citizens and enterprises. The table below shows the number of heterogeneous projects presented for each category of services (source: CRC Italy).

In Italy, if we weigh the degree of e-government deployment against the investments carried out over the past decade, the result is not very reassuring. Certainly, much interest has arisen on the issue, but the hoped-for overturning of the relationship between paper and digital practices has not yet taken place, even when possibilities have been maximised by public authorities by means of their web portals. It is likely that the physiologically slow manifestation of the effects of most technological innovations has had a braking effect. However, we cannot deny that even when Italian public administrations succeed in offering on-line services, users adopt them with a certain delay compared to the European average. This is partly due to some factors which are peculiar to our country, such as the tendency to prefer a direct relationship with the competent civil servant, and maybe also some wariness about procedures that are devoid of a certain degree of subjectivity. In a country like Italy, which has a limited penchant for scientific-technological culture, we also have to come to terms with a diffused conservative attitude described as "anxiety caused by incapacity to understand"[51]. However, if we put ourselves in the shoes of the user, we realise that many of the on-line services offered by public administrations are actually difficult to use. This is even more obvious if, in a comparative approach, we see for example how easily we can buy things on eBay[52].

(51) Granelli A. (edited by), "Comunicare l'innovazione. Perché il successo del nuovo dipende dalla capacità di spiegarlo", ed. Il Sole 24 Ore, Milan, 2005 (*Communicating innovation. Because the success of innovations depends on the ability to explain them*)

(52) Ebay is a Californian company who immediately understood that the key to internet development does not lie in the creation of commercial spaces that are a copy of existing ones, but rather in the creation of social spaces for interpersonal communication, which can also be used for commercial applications but cannot be reduced to them.

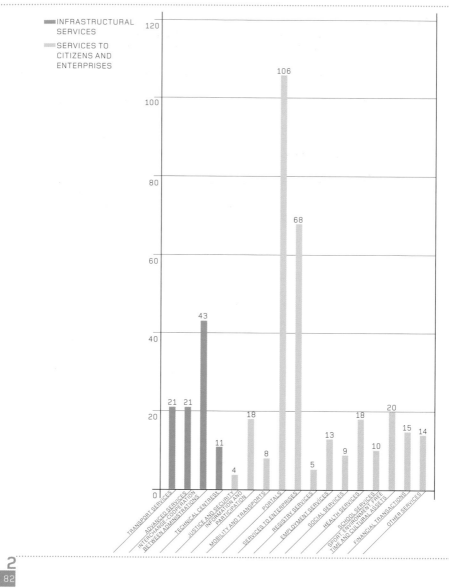

- INFRASTRUCTURAL SERVICES
- SERVICES TO CITIZENS AND ENTERPRISES

120

106

100

80

68

60

43

40

21 21

20 18 18 20
13 15 14
11 10
8 9
4 5

0

TRANSPORT SERVICES
ADVANCED SERVICES
INTERCHANGE COOPERATION BETWEEN ADMINISTRATIONS
TECHNICAL CENTRES
JUSTICE AND SECURITY INFORMATION AND PARTICIPATION
MOBILITY AND TRANSPORTS
PORTALS
SERVICES TO ENTERPRISES
REGISTRY SERVICES
EMPLOYMENT SERVICES
SOCIAL SERVICES
HEALTH SERVICES
SCHOOL SERVICES
SPORT ENVIRONMENT FREE TIME AND CULTURAL ASSETS
FINANCIAL TRANSACTIONS
OTHER SERVICES

6. Digital urban planning

6.1 Digital life

In western societies, ICT permeates today all aspects of social life, inducing even considerable changes in relationships and individual behaviours.

Network infrastructures cover the entirety of most urbanised territories.

The "digital life" phenomenon affects all young generations who, in addition to school training on computer utilisation, have developed new codes of social interactions using cell phones, PCs, interactive television and other digital multimedia devices currently available on the market (smart phone, videophones, palmtops, i-pod, etc.).

Networking has become the new reference for social organisation[53].

Cell phones are a sort of "security blanket" making young people feel more reassured as they are always available, they are always connected to a network of relationships linking them to their peers[54]. A study carried out at the *London School of Economics* in 2006 shows that 91% of UK youths above 12 years of age have a cell phone. However, the most interesting finding is that all the interviewees admitted feeling extremely frustrated and excluded from social life if nobody gets in touch with them, especially via SMS[55].

Technology is clearly becoming the preferred system for social communication, changing individual behaviours and group interactions within settlements, and consequently transforming the ways in which cities are used.

The same study shows that more than one third of European citizens between 16 and 24 years of age use mobile phones to surf the internet or check their e-mails, and in some cases this use of cell phones is dominant compared to the normal function of the device, i.e. voice communication.

Moreover, the same population cohort spends on average 13 hours per week on internet and 48% of them use it every day.

Young Europeans, regardless of their school education, are particularly inclined to use ICT and their capacity will soon close the generational Digital Divide which still concerns some of their parents.

Thus, the familiarity of new generations with the use of new technologies represents an important factor that will drive modern society towards a model of Digital Life, which will lay the foundations for future processes of territorial transformation, as well as for innovative procedures required to govern them.

(53) see Castells M., "The Network Society: A Cross-Cultural Perspective". cit.

(54) see Fistola R., "Digital urban planning e pianificazione digitale del territorio", cit. (*Digital urban planning and territorial digital planning*)

(55) see Carphone Warehouse, "The Mobile life Survey Report 2006", London School of Economics and Political Science, http://www.mobilelife2006.co.uk

hTC TyTN II

6.2 Digital plan

We have repeatedly highlighted how the spread of ICTs is profoundly changing relational models and many activities in mostly advanced societies, from *home banking* to *e-commerce*, from e-government to *on-line trading*, etc. However, in urban planning and in the management of territorial and urban transformation processes, a certain initial reticence seems to hamper the fine-tuning of new instruments and methodologies.

Currently, territorial management processes do not use ICTs to their full potential. We can identify the following levels of ICT application: representative level, additional level, instrumental level, complying level[56].

At the representative level, ICTs are used to create new territorial representation methodologies. This includes both technical representation components, which are being revolutionised by new digital technologies, such as CAD or 3D images, and on-line representation components (web portals).

Technologies can also be added to the territory without necessarily having a structural role. In other words, at the additional level, ICTs are used as innovative systems improving or supporting specific functions that are usually performed in a traditional way.

For instance, functions of traffic control or urban surveillance, traditionally performed by municipal police, can be carried out by digital systems using video-cameras appropriately installed in "sensitive" areas of the city.

The third level has been defined "instrumental". Here, technology is considered as a useful instrument to gain new territorial knowledge through innovative HW/SW environments.

From a technical point of view, the use of GIS as an instrument to gain new territorial knowledge can be a good example.

Just like from a telematic point of view, e-government services can be a useful and innovative instrument to carry out different administrative tasks.

Although very interesting, the complying level is generally little exploited. In this particular case, ICTs guarantee the compliance of territorial transformation management by redefining its phases. In technical terms, this level includes all the new instruments that are capable of completely re-engineering the planning process. Examples are the "communities" or "fora" that stimulate on-line participation to decision-making and territorial management processes.

E-PLANNING 2

(56) see Fistola R., "Digital urban planning e pianificazione digitale del territorio", cit. (Digital urban planning and territorial digital planning)

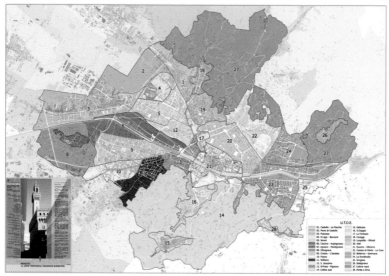

1. Digital map of the "Elementary Organic Territorial Units" from the Structural Plan of the City of Florence (2007)

All of the above-mentioned ICT application levels can contribute to elaborating a new generation of urban planning instruments suited to manage future territorial transformations by making the most out of technological innovations: the Digital Plans.

The elaboration of territorial transformation projects can be divided in three phases: knowledge acquisition, decision-making, implementation and effect monitoring.

Applied to a traditional Urban Plan, the first phase corresponds to urban analyses and their representation, the second to the elaboration of Plan tables and technical implementation standards, the third phase corresponds to its approval and management.

Let us see now how these three phases can be applied to a Digital Plan.

We will make a distinction between those operations which have undergone (even considerable) changes in their transfer from traditional to digital methodologies, and those which, on the contrary, are exclusively ICT-enabled and therefore represent an even higher level of innovation.

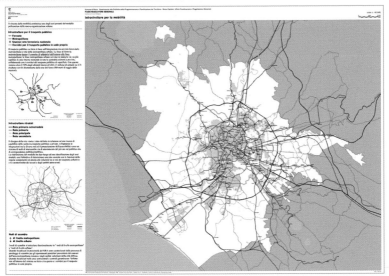

2. Digital map of the "Mobility Infrastructures" from the General Town Planning Scheme" of the City of Rome (2003)

6.3 Knowledge acquisition

The phase of knowledge acquisition is most sensitive to technological innovations. Some methodologies have been completely revolutionised by the introduction of computers and the spread of digital networks. Others are ICT-enabled and therefore appeared with those networks. We will now try to mention some of the elements contributing to knowledge acquisition, describing methodologies before and after the IT revolution.

Basic cartography – The cartographic resources of Italian local authorities are often outdated and important territorial changes are not represented in their maps. Prior to any Plan-related operation, it is therefore necessary to obtain updated versions of the cartography and of the set of aerial photos concerning the territory under exam. This phase has always been very expensive and time-consuming: calling upon a specialised company for the cartography updating, organising flights under favourable weather conditions, elaborating geographical references for the final drawing up of maps and for their reproduction. For some time now, the cartographic material of local authorities has been elaborated on a digital support, thus facilitating archiving and reproduction processes and speeding up updating processes. Moreover, internet has made the distribution of cartographic material a much easier process.

Today, local authorities have specific institutional websites providing stakeholders with different scales of cartographies of the territories under their competence: from basic maps to thematic ones and to those of the General Town Planning Scheme.

Long gone are the times when a professional requesting, for example, some maps of the general town planning scheme was obliged to go to the competent municipal office, ask for a form, make a bank transfer, go back to the same office with a proof of payment, introduce a request and wait for the print to be made (the printing was often outsourced to an external office that generally took its time). Today, the professional can identify him/herself on the Municipality website and download the relevant maps directly on his/her PC. This also applies to Municipalities located thousands of miles away from his/her place of residence!

Aerial photographs – Websites like *Google Earth*[57] or *Live Search*[58] offer an exhaustive coverage of zenith aerial photographs of our planet. In mostly urbanised areas, the high resolution of photographs makes it possible to distinguish cars or even human profiles. In the most densely populated areas, *Live Search* offers a close bird's eye perspective from the four cardinal points, which means that for every single building we can have the representation of the four different façades. In urban planning, this function enables us to perform operations which in the past would have only been possible after a series of thorough on-the-spot investigations: number of building levels, building typology, chromatic features, building additions, infringement of building regulations, etc.

Computer Aided Design – The use of CAD for the elaboration of Plan Tables has generated a series of important benefits. Firstly, it has made it possible to use particularly effective colour legends, especially for representations, such as land zoning, using a very high number of legend headings. In the past, it was necessary to fabricate "unstable" transparencies full of sticking halftone screens of different sizes that only allowed for black and white reproductions. However, CAD tools have become an indispensable instrument in urban planning thanks to their calculating capacity and their ability to easily modify tables. We all remember spending entire nights calculating the allocations of urban

(57) http://earth.google.it
(58) http://maps.live.it

1. Satellite image of the Pentagon, from Google Earth

standards with the triangulation method, and repeating those calculations every time the draft Plan was modified.

3D Simulations – Before the computer era, the 3D representation of draft Plans was realised by the most skilful collaborators, endowed with rare abilities and capable of elaborating complex bird's eye perspectives which, sometimes, could even acquire considerable artistic value. It is understood that those elaborations were the result of many hours of hard work and therefore existed in limited numbers. Sometimes, they were even unique. 3D modelling has turned a whole generation of very young professionals into project communicators. If used skilfully, 3D software has an extraordinary simulation capacity, which has quickly become fundamental to assess the insertion of projects in the context of reference and evaluate their impact. The great advantage is given by the possibility to move freely within the project in a virtual environment reproducing the real world.

Sensors and detection stations - Real time data collection on traffic, availability of parking space, indicators of air and noise pollution etc. are all data that can determine relevant territorial strategies: traffic ban along specific road axes, for example, or the planning of new segments.

This wide range of data and the capacity to simulate the effectiveness of transformations during their planning phase (e.g. traffic models) are only possible thanks to new technologies. Nothing like that was possible in the past.

Geographic Information System – Additional levels of territorial knowledge are possible thanks to the GIS, which functions as a daily working tool for administrations, citizens, authorities and businesses. A GIS concentrates data management and data distribution and consultation in the same environment.

It is at the same time an informative tool for citizens and a shared workspace for public administrations, where different offices can consult, add or edit data. The aim is to organise and make accessible information and documents that would otherwise remain scattered among different offices and authorities. Once more, this is only possible thanks to ICTs.

E-government - The computerisation of public administration makes it possible to process documents and manage procedures through digital systems, thanks to information and communication technologies. The results can be appreciated in the speeding up of administrative work and in the offer of faster services for citizens and enterprises, through the web portals of the relevant administrations.

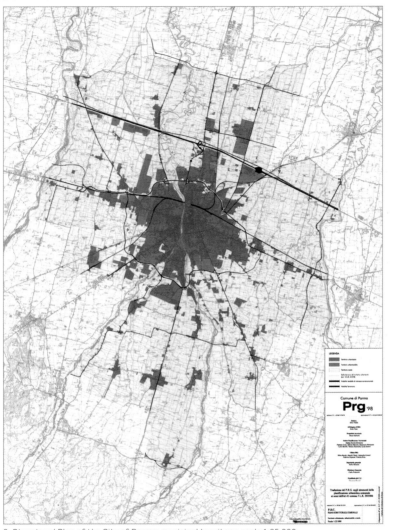

2. Structural Plan of the City of Parma: municipal territory, scale 1:25.000

3. 3D models of a historic centre

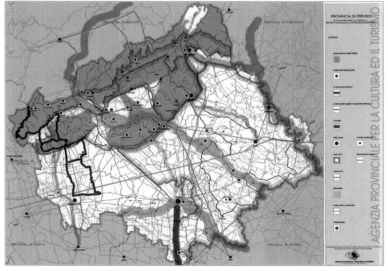

4. Thematic map from the GIS of the province of Treviso

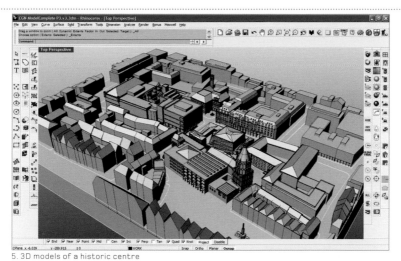

5. 3D models of a historic centre

6. Aerial photograph of a Seattle neighbourhood, from Live Search

6.4 Decision-making

So far, the role of ICTs in decision-making has been less visible. Considerable improvements are particularly noticeable in citizens' participation in choices being made. The complexity of current social systems has strengthened the role of territorial local stakeholder while enfeebling the representativeness of political parties and trade unions. At the same time, direct forms of social representation, such as neighbourhood committees, environmental movements, consumers' group, youth movements, NGOs, and other entities pursuing specific sectorial objectives, have grown stronger. In participated urban planning, local institutions are oriented towards a form of territorial management involving all stakeholders (governance), utilising open, adjustable and reversible systems.

Traditional political arenas, such as municipal, regional and provincial councils, are assisted by informal orientation groups, including social tables, neighbourhood workshops and study groups, whose aim is to compare territorial interests in a direct manner. Representative democracy will then decide whether to transpose or not the indications thus provided (*bottom- up*).

Internet can considerably support these forms of democratic participation to the political debate, by spreading information among citizens and, at the same time, activating the opposite process, i.e. the active contribution of citizens to the debate and to the shaping of political choices and institutional orientations.

Fora and Chat - Typical internet tools, such as *Fora and Chat*, can be used to that purpose[59]. These are IT platforms containing discussions and messages posted by users on specific topics. Entire virtual communities of regular users that meet and discuss in asynchronous (forum) or synchronous way (chat) appear and develop around these platforms. A moderator, who activates the discussion and ensures its conformity with predefined rules, is generally in charge of their coordination. If used for conflict resolution within specific methodologies, they can help solve NIMBY phenomena stemming from protests of Neighbourhood Committees[t].

On-line polls - On-line polls are another typical internet instrument that can support participated planning by directly showing the degree of satisfaction with ongoing decisions. If organised prior to specific interventions, they can be very useful orientation instruments in trying to meet, as far as possible, the desires of the people concerned by the decision.

(59) see Caddy J., "Citizens as Partners: Information, Consultation and Public Participation in Policy-Making", OECD Publishing, Paris 2001.
(60) see Della Porta D., "Comitati di cittadini e democrazia urbana", (*Citizens committees and urban democracy*) Rubettino ed., Catanzaro 2004.

1. Association of some quantitative parameters on the digital cartography of a GIS

Geographic Information System – To elaborate the choices of urban planning instruments, the most widespread application of a GIS is the realisation of an "intelligent" digital cartography capable of connecting spatial coordinates with the multitude of parameters expressed by the territory.

The concept at the heart of their technology is the possibility to connect "positions" with "information", analyse, question and view the different informative levels in an intuitive manner, trying to understand their correlations and foresee possible evolutions. The scope of application can range from territorial and urban planning itself to public health, tax control, civil protection, service network management, etc., embracing both the public and private sector.

Participated approach – This is another aspect of participated planning, as we have described it so far, i.e. the relationship between public decision-making bodies and intervention proposals voiced by private operators. This approach stems from the assumption that the public-private relationship is guided (rather than imposed) by public administration on the basis of a predefined set of clear, fair and transparent rules[61].

This is to ensure the feasibility of planned interventions according to the urban planning instrument, by verifying that Plan forecasts are compatible with the interests of private operators. Being aware of the intentions of property owners, communicating with them on the basis of carefully established "game rules" can be very useful not only to ensure the feasibility of interventions but also to obtain consensus. To this end, ICTs can be very useful by creating specific IT platforms aimed at managing the public-private relationship by facilitating the spread of initiatives, the presentation of proposals in standardised formats, the on-line interaction with process managers, etc.

Observations Counter-deductions – The so-called Observations and Counter-deductions, and more generally the approval of a Plan, can be managed through appropriate on-line databases. Besides making archiving and consultation easier than in a paper archive, observations can be organised through "metadata"[62] with different labelling and classification modalities.

This makes it easier to compare different groups of observations, for instance, to make sure that similar behaviours are adopted in similar situations. Finally, counter-indications can be published on-line for greater administrative transparency.

6.5 Monitoring of effects

The implementation and monitoring of urban plans over time has always been the weakest link of planning processes. We have obtained our diploma in Architectural studies after studying "model" Plans in sector specific magazines which described innovative procedures and methodologies, captivating project experiences and complex equalisation mechanisms. Plans were described by the authors themselves, with all the emphatic drive and scientific utopia that one can reasonably expect to find in the words of an author who is called to describe his own work. Since the date of publication often coincided with the project submission to Administrations, Plans were described exactly

(61) see Fusero P., "Il rapporto pubblico privato nel PRG: pratiche contesti e nuovi orizzonti", (*The relationship between the public and the private sector in the General Town Planning Scheme: practices, contexts and new horizons*) Palombi ed., Rome 2004.
(62) A metadatum (from the Greek *meta*- "beyond, after" and the Latin *datum* "information"- plural: *data*), literally "datum over a (different) datum", is a piece of information describing a set of data. A typical example of metadata is the information sheet of a library catalogue. It contains information about the content, the author, the modality of access and the location of the book, i.e. all the data concerning the book.he main function of a metadata system is to facilitate research and allow for interoperability in different fields thanks to a series of equivalences between the describing elements.

as they had been conceived by the authors, rather than as they would appear following amendments by the Municipal Consultative Council, remarks by citizens and authorities, counter-deductions by the Offices and changes by the Higher Authority. After a difficult approval process (which can even involve thousands of observations and last for many years), a plan can lose a great part of its initial innovative drive.

The management phase can then completely thwart the initial good intentions of project makers, by constraining Plans in a rigid process that does not allow for any change, unless formerly agreed upon by the exasperating Institute of Variants. General Town Planning Scheme lack flexibility and are unable to quickly adjust to the rapid changes of modern society. This is why, at the beginning of the eighties, an attitude of mistrust arose in the wake of the so-called "deregulation", when the procedural slowness of the Plan was opposed to the agility of the Project[63].

Today, some people still have doubts about the necessity for a General Town Planning Scheme and quite often local Administrations prefer to resort to Complex Programmes of doubtful public utility, rather than initiating the long (nobody knows how long) process of Town planning scheme elaboration.

Monitoring the effects produced by the instruments in use is not common practice in urban planning. It is as if the efforts of public administrations were just limited to the elaboration of urban planning instruments, paying little interest to the measurement of their efficiency over time in order to fix possible problems. Apart from some university studies[64], very few and little meaningful practical applications exist.

How can ICTs be applied to the implementation and monitoring of urban planning instruments? Suggestions for a productive use of new information and communication technologies are quite dim. It is even difficult to identify traditional consolidated methodologies on these objectives. Let us try to identify some arguments and describe them in an attempt to outline some possible research paths, bearing in mind that we are still at an experimental stage.

Technical Implementation Norms – The issue of TIN flexibility, within the framework of legal certainty which must in any case be ensured, has always fascinated sector workers. Nevertheless, it is difficult to identify meaningful experiences in this field. In principle, TINs have become more geared towards the achievement of predefined objectives

(63) Indovina F., "Strategie e soggetti per la trasformazione urbana, anni '80", (*Strategies and stakeholders for urban transformation, the 80s*) in F. Indovina (edited by) *La città occasionale*, F. Angeli, Milan 1993.
(64) Tutino A., "L'efficacia del Piano, (*The effectiveness of the Plan*), Casa, Città, Territorio, Rome 1986.

in terms, for instance, of public service provision. Once specific categories of public services have achieved an optimal level, land destination and urban planning requirements resulting from new construction settlements could be diverted towards other forms of public utility. A GIS could easily measure the degree of achievement of quantitative objectives and suitable on-line polls or *ad hoc* fora could help identify compensation forms that best match citizens' needs.

Fabricability performance indicators – Indicators of buildings' fabricability could take into account their performance, such as their energy efficiency or bio-architectural standards.

The lower the consumption of energy, the higher the fabricability bonus within established limits. A GIS could even contain interactive windows where stakeholders, by introducing a series of pre-defined performance variables, can see how volumetric indexes in a specific homogeneous area increase or decrease according to the additional qualitative performance assigned to the construction settlement they intend to achieve.

Equalisation models – Permutation processes of equalisation models could be coordinated by an automated system contained in the GIS which would be capable of indicating the availability of suitable parcels or the interests of building plots' owners in these permutation processes. Local authorities could thus facilitate permutation operations and, at the same time, create an urbanisation hierarchy by stipulating, for instance, that a specific area cannot start building until an adjacent area has achieved complete saturation (or a fixed percentage of built surface). A GIS, consultable by all regularly authorised stakeholders, could directly manage process monitoring and all the relevant information.

Variant requests – Quite often, after a few years of General Town Planning Scheme management, a considerable number of variant requests can start piling up. Sometimes the "pressure" exerted by those requests spurs public authorities to review the General Town Planning Scheme in force.

An accurate classification of variant requests could be a useful tool providing the new town planning scheme designer with a clear picture of the situation and with additional food for thought. Of course, they represent a limited aspect of the issue, they represent specific interests and are to a large extent unacceptable, after a careful analysis. Nevertheless, their usefulness is twofold: firstly, recurrent specific requests provide the possibility to identify possible critical aspects of the scheme in force. Secondly, mapping variant requests provides an idea of the distribution on the territory of the urban "tension" and thus gives an overview of owners' expectations and, in some cases, of their intervention proposals. It is important to provide this phase with an institutional framework by creating an ad hoc structure, such as a specific bureau, an agency or another body internal to the Plan office.

The collection of intervention proposals should be systematic in order to allow for true databases to be set up. To this purpose, digital networks and new information and communication technologies are obviously very useful.

Content-wise, this is not something new, since traditionally private individuals have always had the possibility to submit intervention proposals to the administration, through observations or other informal means. Nonetheless, this is a new element of paramount importance from a formal perspective: it is no longer about showing a dissenting opinion with administration choices, but about participating to a public-private process that makes the plan more flexible throughout its management.

Procedure monitoring – Normally, the validation of a building procedure involves receiving opinions from different offices with competences in this field (traffic, urban planning networks, private building sector, parks and public gardens, etc.) and different authorities. By appointing the Unique Project Manager and by setting up the Services Conference, public administrations have opted for greater transparency and less complexity in their relationship with citizens and enterprises. This could be further improved thanks to the use of a GIS allowing for procedural developments to be monitored on-line directly from the computer at home.

Applicants can therefore check procedural developments and be informed about the requests made by different offices, in other words, they can closely monitor, step by step, the validation process of their construction projects and be directly informed of any possible hitches.

Detection stations – The management of urban planning instruments goes well beyond the administrative component. For instance, specific systems of digital sensors can monitor parameters such as pollution indicators, building heat loss coefficients, traffic conditions, availability of parking space, etc.

All these data can be processed by specific stations which, according

1. Detection and video-surveillance sensors powered by solar energy

to their detections, can then take specific measures such as blocking traffic in a given urban area, diverting vehicles towards alternative routes, providing information to travellers, providing suitable security measures in restricted areas, etc.

Parking - A system of sensors and video-cameras provides information on the availability of parking space in the city centre. Digital stations monitor the saturation of public and private parking space and send information about free parking space, as well as suggestions on how to get there, to mobile devices available in cars (satellite navigation systems, smart phones, and palmtops).

Traffic - A system of sensors and video-cameras fitted in the most sensitive urban areas elaborates data on traffic and bottlenecks. Besides communicating to variable message panels located along access infrastructures, it also sends information to mobile devices available in cars suggesting alternative routes and travel time.

Digital road - Sections of infrastructures connected to the city give the possibility to increase the number of lanes giving access to or departing from the city centre, change one-way signs, close/open road sections according to the time slot and the traffic conditions detected by the digital monitoring system.

2. New York traffic monitoring room

E-CITIES 3

7. Cities of the future

In this third part of the book, we will focus on the future of cities with a view to digital networks and ICT applications development. We will look into the concept of *Digital City* analysing the different meanings it is acquiring in the international scientific community. They all conjure up images of highly impressive scenarios, but normally refer to more or less sophisticated, friendly, interaction-oriented hardware/software architectures providing information and services to citizens in various fields: tourism, trade, transport, welfare, health, civil protection, politics, etc., in other words, Civil Networks[65]. Frankly, we are interested in something more!

7.1 Digital Cities

Digital Cities are often associated with an arena where people from a local community can interact and exchange knowledge, experiences, services, or simply share interests through internet[66]. Examples are the American On Line (AOL) Digital Cities. These are on-line guides of major American cities where, besides comprehensive information on entertainment and touristic activities (restaurants, attractions, cinemas, etc.), the user has the possibility to purchase services and products on-line.

More complex are experiences like the *Amsterdam Digital City*, which appears like a hardware/software platforms allowing citizens to interact with the public administration in order to obtain services or information, using the pc at home, but also from other locations in public places (libraries, bus stops, etc.)[67]. The *Helsinki Arena Project* is even more diverse.

It creates a virtual city using a 3D model and allows for the interaction of citizens through *live videos*[68].

The *Kyoto Digital City* is a complex architecture on three *layers* which is capable of creating synergies and providing citizens and tourists with a lot of information and services obtained from the GIS, such as real time data collected by detection centres scattered throughout the city (traffic, parking capacity, weather, pollution, etc.)[69].

Although rich of innovative elements, these examples of Digital Cities are solely limited to the technical aspects of the hardware/software platforms that convey them: Digital City = Virtual City.

The objective is to represent the city, its functions and, where possible, its interactions in a virtual arena created through ICTs[70].

Interesting, but certainly well below our objectives!

We are more interested in expanding the concept of Digital City and

(65) The "Civic Network" is a telematic portal promoted by the public administration and endowed with communication, information and service functions for the benefit of citizens. The existing ones embrace both e-government aspects (on-line services offered by public administrations) and e-governance aspects (citizens' discussion fora, direct participation to the life of the local community). Iperbole, created in Bologna in 1995, is one of the first Civic Networks in Europe.
(66) see Ishida T., "Understanding Digital Cities: Cross-Cultural Perspectives", cit.

1. Carlorattiassociati, Digital Water Pavilion Zaragoza, 2007

associate it with a city of the future (a real city, not a virtual one) where the intensive use of digital networks and ICTs can produce considerable changes in the way in which the city is used, as well as in social interactions, functions distribution and spatial set-up. In our case, considerations on the issue of digital cities by authors like W.J. Mitchell or M. Castells, who have developed important research on the sociological effects of a future dominated by ICT, are much more stimulating.

(67) see Van den Besselaar P. and Beckers D., op.cit.
(68)ee Linturi R., Koivunen M. and Sulkanen J., "Helsinki Arena 2000: augmenting a real city to a virtual one", in Digital cities: experiences, technologies and future perspectives, Springer Verlag, New York, 2000.
(69) see Ishida T., "Digital City Kyoto", in t.
(70) see. Aurigi A., "Making the Digital City", Ashgate 2005.

7.2 Fragmentation and Reassembling[71]

The main function of a telecommunication network is to allow humans to interact from a distance. However, not all human activities can be carried out via digital networks. We can perform bank transactions, or shop, or send documents while remaining comfortably seated in front of our computer at home. Yet, if we want to get a trendy haircut, we still need a direct interaction with the hairdresser. If we analyse the effects that the spreading of digital networks is having on our cities, we realise that it is neither a process of centralisation nor of decentralisation of activities, but rather a complex process of "fragmentation" and "reassembling" of existing urban models.

Let us take the effects of on-line book sales through web portals as an example. We notice that choice and purchasing modalities have completely changed compared to the traditional selling patterns of city centre bookstores. Nowadays, choice and purchasing take place in a decentralised way, in the homes and offices of every single buyer. In the past, these activities were concentrated in the city centre, together with all the other operations. Today, they are fragmented and reassembled in homes and work places. At the same time, books are no longer stored in the back-shop of city centre bookstores, but are concentrated in a few large national storage centres located near connection hubs. Proximity to warehouses or buyers is no longer required for back office functions, such as administrative activities and warehouse monitoring: they can be delocalised anywhere and can be carried out at lower costs through tele-working. Distribution and transport patterns have also changed. In the past, books were delivered in considerable quantities to city centre bookstores (which also served as intermediate warehouses) and were then purchased by buyers. Today, with on-line shopping, attention is focused on how rapidly the parcel is delivered from the central warehouse to the homes of buyers scattered throughout the territory.

If we apply this type of analysis to different types of on-line sales and services, the results can be very different due to the specific nature of the product or service offered. Books take up little space and have a very high commercial value, they are not perishable and delivery times of a couple of days are generally well accepted by buyers. This makes it possible to create considerable economies of scale by concentrating warehousing services in a few national storage centres. Moreover, books do not have to be "tried on" to see how they look, or "touched"

(71) Here, I retrace the train of thought followed by W.J. Mitchell in the chapter "Designing the Digital City", in: AAVV, *Digital City*, Springer Berlin, Berlin 2000.

to verify their consistency, or "smelled" to appreciate their scent. Generally, before purchasing a book, we can simply consult specialised websites to obtain detailed information or reviews in order to make an informed choice. The same reasoning applies to electronic equipment and many other similar items.

But as far as foodstuffs are concerned, the situation is very different. Foodstuffs have a lower commercial value than books, they are perishable, and their organoleptic characteristics cannot be assessed on-line before purchasing them. Delivery times of two-three days, which are acceptable for books, are not suitable for foodstuffs. Foodstuffs therefore need regional rather than national distribution centres. If we take a hot pizza, things are even more complicated: immediate delivery times are imperative. Otherwise, the product will lose its quality and will be impossible to sell.

Software, music CDs, videos, etc. require an opposite reasoning. They can be chosen, tested, sold and delivered directly on-line thanks to a good digital network. The localisation of distribution centres has no constraints at all and can be anywhere on the planet. In this particular case, ICTs completely revolutionise goods distribution systems and go as far as replacing them.

The development of ICTs does not simply have repercussions on goods sales and distribution systems. It also affects the planning of working spaces.

Let us try to compare the traditional model of office and all its related functions with the new model resulting from a diffused use of networks and digital services. Traditional management offices provide individual working spaces connected both to common areas containing technical equipment (photocopying machines, printers, plotters, fax, etc.) and to conference and meeting rooms. Access is regulated by the reception, while distribution and circulation are organised as to ensure maximum efficiency levels for the interactions taking place within the building. These buildings are typically located either in the city centre with good public transport connections, or in the outskirts of the city, ensuring a qualitative building complex with access and parking facilities.

The development of ICTs does not simply result in office space relocation, but it fragments, redistributes and recombines it with other activities. In the era of computers, e-mails and digital telephone services, office space no longer needs to be concentrated in specialised buildings, but it can be distributed across houses located in different neighbourhoods or other decentralised spaces. When documents are in a digital format and are stored in on-line archives, the employee no longer needs to be physically close to them.

Equipment such as photocopying machines and printers become smaller and less expensive since they are fitted in the houses of tele-workers, and anyway paper copies of documents are no longer necessary as they used to be in the past. The most evident result of this digital revolution is the combination of working space with other spaces: with the home environment first of all, but also with hotel rooms, equipped with broadband internet connections and desks for clients' notebooks, with airport waiting rooms providing suitable wireless connections, even with planes providing passengers with power and network cables.

This process of work decentralisation implies a less intensive use of office space in the city business districts, which can thus be reconsidered for more flexible uses. Of course, gatherings and face-to-face meetings are irreplaceable for several reasons and their spaces in buildings and offices will therefore remain and could indeed be enriched with catering services and short stay facilities. It is also foreseeable that hotels, airports, congress centres and other venues for service-sector activities will also make arrangements to host short-time business meetings and gatherings. In this new context, software and systems of sensors and video-cameras can easily ensure surveillance operations.

For all these reasons, the link of physical proximity, which had bound together the different components of traditional offices, is weakened or even broken, and individual components can be used in a flexible way. Localisation of space for tele-work is much more flexible and makes it possible to carry out most of the workload directly from home, thus reducing home-to-work travel.

Similar analyses could be applied to many activities within schools, universities, hospitals, research centres, etc. But of course, many aspects of education or health care still require face-to-face interaction and will increasingly tend to converge in urban centres in order to create economies of scale.

New scenarios, some of which depend on the different population groups, will also characterise residential spaces. For wealthier social classes, the ICT revolution means getting rid of traditional space and time constraints due to business commitments and opening towards greater flexibility and independence: a famous writer, for instance, can decide to live in one of the most beautiful places on earth without losing contact with the external world thanks to digital networks. A university professor can chose to live in the countryside, away from urban chaos, in a high-tech cottage equipped with the most recent ICT innovations. The same applies to translators. For many years, I had a Canadian translator, whom I never met personally, and I never knew where she was when she was translating my texts, since she had several residences around the world.

The processes of fragmentation and reassembling that we have just described can induce new neighbouring relationships which are worth considering. Cities built during the industrial era have led to a rigid separation between different functional areas (zoning): residential areas, productive areas, business districts, commercial areas, etc. Since the industrial revolution in the mid-XVIII century, demographic growth and all the problems related to the mixing of domestic and productive functions have progressively pushed residential neighbourhoods away from working areas, thus producing commuting phenomena which, in the most apparent cases, have reached a few hours of travelling per day. The result has been the creation of "dormitory" neighbourhoods which, even in the most comfortable circumstances (like the *garden cities* revolving around big American or English cities), are abandoned by the resident population during most of the day.

Thanks to ICTs and tele-working, working spaces can be fragmented and recombined with domestic spaces in residential neighbourhoods, thus creating new patterns of territorial use resembling those of the pre-industrial era. An increasing portion of the population has the possibility to spend most of the day in the neighbourhood where he/she resides, and which has become his/her main working place. The connotation of "dormitory neighbourhood" can thus disappear and transformations can begin to take place: more public services, childcare services, new commercial activities, bars, gyms, hairdressers, etc.

Public spaces and streets are also reorganised in order to be more alive during the day with entertainment spaces, parks, resting and leisure areas, and greater attention is paid to urban quality. The result is amazing! Face-to-face interactions in residential neighbourhoods increase thanks to the deployment of digital networks. A superfluous analysis of the ICT phenomenon would have suggested exactly the opposite.

The *t* are somehow an example of this model. The wooden houses inspired by traditional Japanese architecture are recovered to fulfil working and domestic functions, attracting new dwellers (often teleworkers) and therefore favouring the development of many new local services and commercial activities.

7.3 Digital ecology

It would be now interesting to apply the anticipated effects of ICT development on future urban models, in a reasonable perspective of environmental, social and economic sustainability. To do so, we can draw on the considerations expressed by W.J. Mitchell in *E-topia*[72], starting from the five points which he identifies as being crucial for the "digital revolution": Dematerialisation, Demobilisation, Mass Customisation, Intelligent Operation, Soft Transformation.

Dematerialisation - When a new system based on digital technologies replaces one which is indeed based on physical interactions, as in complex home-banking and e-government processes, or even in simple e-mails, there is an effect of dematerialisation: physical objects are turned into virtual objects. Generally, this saves a lot of money and time. A paper letter sent through traditional postal services requires paper consumption, a postman coming to collect it, a post office at the point of origin sorting the correspondence, a vehicle delivering it to the post office at the point of destination (sometimes a plane is required), and another postman bringing the letter to the home of the addressee. An incredible waste of time and money compared to an e-mail! Not to mention all the pollution produced: from the cutting down of the tree used to produce the paper, to the exhaust fumes of the postal worker's scooter. Up to a few years ago, the frontier of architectural sustainable development was the so-called "bio-architecture"[73]: given the fact that physical constructions are unavoidable, the most reasonable ecological objective is to make them as efficient as possible. In the future, new ICTs will enable us to put the issue in different terms: is it really necessary to build this new building? Can we partially or totally replace the functions that it should host with digital systems? Can we optimise the use of already existing buildings?

Demobilisation - Resources can also be saved when the need to commute, especially for work, is partially or totally replaced by telepresence (video-conferences, e-learning platforms, chat, VOIP, smart phone, webcam, e-mail, etc.). Moving bits of data is certainly much easier and cheaper than moving people or goods. Savings derive from reduced fuel consumption for transport, reduced pollution and travel expenses, but also from the limitation of travel time, which is often longer than effective working time. Naturally, human interactions are so complex that it would be silly to believe that they can be totally replaced by digital networks: the key to our reasoning is how we can benefit from telecommunications to create more efficient urban models.

[72] see Mitchell W.J., "E-topia: Urban Life, Jim – But Not As We Know It", MIT Press 1999.
[73] "Bio-architecture" encompasses all the disciplines that carry out ecologically sustainable behaviors in the face of natural and anthropogenic ecosystems. Some of the basic planning-related principles of bio-architecture are the optimisation of the relationship between buildings and the context in which they are inserted, the protection of ecosystems, the use of natural materials and resources, the non-production of harmful emissions, the use of renewables, the use of eco-compatible materials and construction techniques, etc.

New policies discouraging the use of private vehicles could favour this process. Nowadays, different categories of workers, especially those with part-time or with flexible and changing daily commitments, work directly from their homes through digital networks, have flexible working hours and commute to their working place for specific meetings or courses, only for a couple of hours a day, and only a few days a week. This reduces considerably overall traffic volumes, as well as daily peak-hours, and contributes to reducing the negative effects of home-to-work travel including the separation of domestic and work environment that was typical of the industrial era. The resulting urban model is a multi-centred city made of multifunctional neighbourhoods, which are self-sufficient on a pedestrian level, interconnected via appropriate public transport networks and efficient digital networks. Weighing the functional mixture of domestic spaces, working spaces and services to people can help strike the right balance between pedestrian movement, mechanic transport and telecommunications.

Mass Customisation - Besides dematerialisation of physical objects and the reduction of home-to-work travel, the *new economy* of the future will be based on the personalisation of objects, spaces and services. During the industrial era, economic development was focused on the standardisation of production processes. In the era of deverticalisation[74], companies will try to develop increasingly flexible products capable of satisfying the growing demand for personalised products and services, which will become a fundamental added-value in advanced economies. Even everyday objects will be personalised to the benefit of every user. In the morning, we all read the newspaper, but it is unlikely that we read all its pages. As opposed to a paper copy, an electronic newspaper can be personalised by highlighting only the topics that bear a certain interest for a given reader, who will then chose whether he/she wants to print the relevant pages or read them from the computer. This translates into less paper (therefore

(74) Per "deverticalizzazione" della produzione si intende che ogni fase del ciclo produttivo viene svolta in uno stabilimento diverso; ognuno di questi stabilimenti è collocato in zone differenti del continente o addirittura del globo, là dove è maggiore la specializzazione in quella fase produttiva e minore il costo della manodopera.

fewer trees to cut down) and less waste (therefore, more savings). Let us now focus on the use of cars in advanced economies. Very often, comfort and the concept of ownership spur us to buy a car for every member of the family, but most of the time these cars remain parked in our garage. If we renounced privately owned cars and if we could count on an "intelligent" car rental system managed through ICTs, the car that we need would always be available: a *Van* for our holidays, a *SUV* for an excursion in the mountains, a *City car* to go shopping in the city centre, a *S.W.* for long journeys, etc. We could thus optimise the use of our car fleet, we would not need to incur purchase expenses, we would have much lower maintenance costs, we would always have new, guaranteed and tailor-made cars for every occasion. Local and national policies could endorse environment-friendly cars and recycle their components in a profitable and sustainable way. Car fleet owners would become private companies operating locally and nationally on behalf of public administrations and infrastructure managing companies, which could in turn become producers of alternative sources of energy fuelling the green engines of cars. By way of example, *Società Autostrade* could install photovoltaic panels along its infrastructures and use the energy thus produced to fuel its car fleet, equipped with sensors and digital stations to assist the driver and reduce accidents, avoid traffic jams, chose alternative routes[75]. Similar benefits could be obtained through the "intelligent" management of public transport services. For instance, if taxis were equipped with satellite detectors and could communicate their position to a digital station, we would automatically receive information on the closest vehicle and on arrival times. Similarly, bus stop panels could indicate waiting times and suggest the best itinerary to get to a desired destination. Transport logistics could also considerably benefit from the use of microchips for the recognition and addressing of goods in order to optimise journeys, reduce storage and speed up delivery.

Intelligent Operation - Intelligence applied to devices providing basic services (water, gas, electricity, telephone, etc.) can contribute to reducing consumption by encouraging savings, especially if this is supported by dynamic pricing policies that stimulate consumption during non-peak hours. Intelligence can also be applied to the operations performed through the provision of the service. Let us take, for example, the act of watering our garden, or a public garden in our city or a ploughed field in the countryside. A non-intelligent watering system obliges the operator to open and close the water tap by turning the

(75) See chapter on "Intelligent Infrastructures".

water hose in the right direction for the required amount of time. A little intelligent automated watering system is equipped with a timer that lets the water out at regular intervals, but it does not take into account whether it is raining or whether there are 40 degrees outside. On the other hand, an intelligent system will be equipped with sensors that check the level of air and soil moisture and activate the system exactly for the necessary time. Similarly, a basic electricity system makes it possible to switch on and off the lights of a house and its electric appliances. A more intelligent system can check the level of temperature and brightness and accordingly switch on the lights and the air-conditioner if it is dark or cold. An even more intelligent system can switch the lights on and off according to the information it receives from a digital station connected to sensors located in every room. Energy will thus be provided only when it is necessary and only if someone is in the room, and electric appliances, such as washing machines or dishwashers, will be activated only during night hours when electricity charges are lowest.

Soft Transformation - In the era of digital networks, the development of new urban models could take advantage of the opportunities arising from dematerialisation processes, from reduced commuting needs and from the personalisation of environments. On a global scale, developed regions will have to adapt existing buildings, urban settlements, open spaces and infrastructures to the new requirements in terms of environmental sustainability and energy efficiency, which were unknown at the time of their realisation. When oil was only a few dozen dollars the barrel and sustainability was not a common concept, car producers could afford to design cars without considering their consumption. But nowadays, no car producer would ever dream of not taking into account fuel efficiency as a priority parameter in the design and marketing of a new model. Moreover, all car producers are working on new prototypes of green cars using alternative propellants other than fossil fuels. The same considerations apply to cities, but with an additional problem: recovering existing buildings and infrastructures. But cities have already undergone similar transformations in the past. During the 20th century, after the world war, industrial cities were deeply renewed in order to face the demand for new industrial areas, new houses for workers, new central offices, transport systems and connecting infrastructures. The cities that were capable of responding to these needs grew faster, the others underwent a slow decline. Nevertheless, territories have paid a very high price for an industrial growth fuelled by fossil fuels. As a result, old neighbourhoods have been abandoned or even knocked down, the historical architectural heritage is at stake, the landscape has been compromised by excessive human intervention, the environment has been disfigured by polluting production waste, infrastructural networks have violently scarred cities and territories, social divisions have multiplied and an increasing percentage of the population can barely scrape a living. Luckily enough, the changes induced by ICTs will not have such devastating effects. Digital networks will have a considerably less invasive environmental impact on the territory than other infrastructures. The rigid functional separation (zoning) has been overcome. Broadband connections will provide today's marginalised territories with an opportunity to be competitive. The emission of polluting agents in the atmosphere will be reduced compared to the industrial era. This will be a gradual process: the transition of cities from what they are to what we want them to be will not be sudden and catastrophic, but it will be slow and incremental.

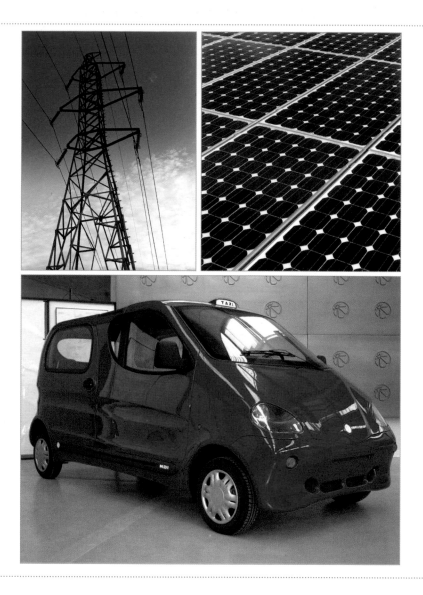

8. Networks and territories of the future

8.1 Infrastructural networks and territorial layers

Over the past fifty years, the relationship between infrastructures and the territory has been constantly evolving. During the post-war reconstruction and the economic boom, important landscape and cultural values were sacrificed in the name of economic development, but in recent years, this relationship has thinned down and is now virtually reduced to the evaluation of environmental impacts. In fact, the relationship between infrastructures and the territory is much more complex, much richer in terms of implications. It is related to economic growth, but also to the protection of social and cultural identities and to the safeguard of landscape and environmental values, both in developed geographical areas and in more vulnerable and remote territories that are cut off from development axes. Public opinion is now convinced that the risk of exclusion should be averted: exclusion from networks, from trade, from development opportunities, which would make it impossible to combine the protection of territorial quality with the conservation of achieved levels of well-being.

Large mobility infrastructures are the development hubs for new economic functions related to globalised exchanges and local territorial dynamics. Airports, vast communication axes, railways and harbours are more than sheer transport infrastructures, they also become driving forces for territorial development. In logistics, the possibility to combine goods movement with more or less complex phases of goods processing would be a real added-value. In this perspective, infrastructural networks (transport but also energy and digital infrastructures) play more than a structural role and function as real drivers generating territorial spin-offs and providing basic conditions for the development of local districts. On the other hand, if we consider cities and urban systems as exchange hubs attracting flows of different natures (goods and people, but also knowledge and know-how), the concept of logistics could be extended to develop the capacities of these systems to turn flows into territorial value[76].

In a globalised world, which is increasingly interdependent but also increasingly destructured and divided, differences between the areas that take part in globalisation and those which are excluded from it become more marked. This can be observed both at a global level, between northern and southern regions of the world, and within the most economically advanced countries, where marginalised areas are doomed to decline since they are not capable of attracting global flows and turning them into local value. Of course, this is not accept-

(76) see Fontana G., "Reti e territori al futuro", Ministry of Infrastructures ed. Rome 2006 (*Future networks and territories*)

able. We cannot accept a constellation of highly integrated excellencies on a global level floating in a sea of marginalised areas, cut off from development and doomed to mediocrity and subsidised economy. We must reconsider many of the current ideas on local development and cohesion policies. To fight against inequalities, we must endorse great territorial projects requiring means and capacities that are hardly available at local level. In this sense, digital networks can play a fundamental role. They can represent the territory as a set of layers and function as connecting threads between the different levels, thus making it possible to intercept flows and turn them into consolidated territorial values.

As described above, space is no longer conceived as a set of local contexts interconnected through infrastructural networks. It is rather the expression of a set of layers, where every hub is a switching and crossing point, a density centre within a gigantic intersection of flows[77]. The traditional concept of *territory-area*, derived from the principle of spatial proximity, is associated with the innovative concept of *territory-hub*, intended as a big hub of intersectorial and multi-scale relationships.

"Territorial platforms" become geographical districts capable of maintaining relationships with big global circuits, thus generating integrated production systems that are able to cope with the challenges of global competition. On the other hand, "territorial hubs" present themselves as being able to favour exchanges between global flows and local territories. They function as incubators capable of multiplying the effects of innovation and extend them to productive and social structures. Finally, "infrastructural connection networks" are a combination of different networks ensuring the circulation of goods and people, but also the swift spread of information and knowledge. This results in air, maritime, rail and road connections, with the corresponding logistic equipment, but also in digital networks integrated with centres of scientific research and the most advanced technological hubs[78].

All the entities that we have identified have a common denominator: the presence of elements capable of attracting flows for the mobility of people, goods and knowledge, combined with some advanced functions. These can be technological hubs and research centres for technological and scientific innovations; schools and universities for the spread of knowledge and the development of specialised skills; service centres for corporate outsourcing[79].

3

118

[77] see Veltz P., "Mondialisation. Villes et territories", Universitaires de France Press, Paris 1996.
[78] see Clementi A., "Corridoi, piattaforme, città senza fine", in Opere pubbliche e città adriatica, AAVV, Actar-D List, Barcelona 2008 (*Corridors, platforms, never-ending cities*)
[79] see Clementi A., "Un avvenire possibile del territorio italiano", in Reti e territori al futuro, Ministry of Infrastructures ed., Rome 2006. (*A possible future for the Italian territory*)

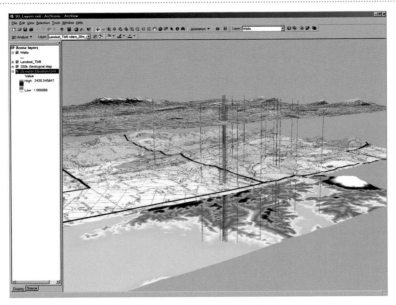

The competitiveness of future territories will also be measured according to their ability to access telecommunication and energy supply networks. The development of renewables, such as wind and photovoltaic energy, will bring production closer to end-users, through a process of local decentralisation, which is also favoured by current policies of increasing liberalisation in these sectors. Mobility, telecommunications and energy networks can therefore be viewed as an infrastructural "unicum" capable of generating important territorial spin-offs, by providing the basic conditions for an "intelligent" development.

8.2 Intelligent territories

In the future, while differences between *rich* and *poor* territories will become less significant, a new distinction will emerge between *intelligent* territories and those which do not have such aptitudes. An "intelligent" territory can apply adequate information and communication technologies within its perimeter in order to maximise efficiency: increase competitiveness while reducing resource consumption.
But what does "being intelligent" mean for a territory?

(80) Here, I follow the train of thought that I already illustrated in chap.3 "Intelligent infra-structures".

There are at least four different ways of applying intelligence to territories[80]: 1) planning territories in an intelligent way; 2) obtaining intelligent information from territories; 3) designing intelligent applications for territories; 4) using territories in an intelligent way.

Planning territories in an intelligent way implies setting up an adequate urban planning scheme capable of creating synergies between different territorial strategies: functional allocation of activities, enhancement of local identities, conservation of landscape and environmental heritage, sustainable economic growth, infrastructure and service provision, contained use of soil, etc. Innovative instruments such as the GIS can support planners in organising data, matching information and simulating the effects of decisions to be taken.

An intelligent territory is capable of providing, through digital networks, information flows that can be processed and used to identify even immediate operational interventions. Systems of sensors can monitor, for instance, natural phenomena such as water levels in water basins or in dams, incipient fires in inaccessible slopes, landslide phenomena in sensitive walls, snowfall levels, leakages in water supply systems, etc. It is also possible to monitor other phenomena related to the functioning of urban areas such as water and air pollution, traffic conditions, the availability of parking space, or the security level in sensitive areas by means of video-cameras and infrared sensor circuits. Through digital networks, all this information can be collected, processed, selected and some of it can even be sent to users, such as information on traffic and parking space, or on waiting times at the stops of public means of transport.

Planning intelligent applications for citizens and enterprises is now an indispensable added-value for the competitiveness of territories. We have already seen that many on-line services can be used as indicators to asses the level of attractiveness of a specific territory: telemedicine, e-government, outsourced corporate services, but also home banking, e-learning, e-commerce, on-line trading, etc. The importance of these applications lies in their ability to induce significant changes in the relationships between stakeholders, thus generating new interaction patterns that are innovative compared to the traditional ones. The list of potential applications of ICTs could be even longer, but the above-mentioned examples are enough to prove that, in order to compete globally, a territory cannot get around the provision of on-line services conveyed by digital networks.

An intelligent use of the territory goes hand in hand with a sustainable

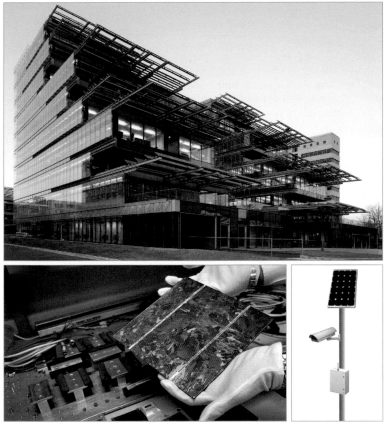

use of its resources. The protection of local identities, especially of marginalised areas, the safeguard of endangered landscape and environmental heritage require adequate telecommunication networks enabling these territories to be connected with global networks. "From marginalised territories to digitalised territories" could be a slogan that sums up in a nutshell sustainable development policies based on the spread of digital networks and on the consequent provision of on-line services to citizens and enterprises in those territories

(80) Seguo qui il filo del ragionamento che ho già condotto nel cap. 3 "infrastrutture intelligenti"

which so far have been left on the verge of economic development, due to negative historical heritage, weak strategies or simply objective natural circumstances. Economically marginalised territories often shelter highly relevant features in terms of landscape (rural areas, mountain regions, islands, small historical centres, etc). The tendency toward depopulation and economic impoverishment, which has characterised these territories over the past thirty years, could be countered through the offer of prominent social and landscape values combined with technological services that are equivalent or even superior to those provided in metropolitan areas. Tele-working, virtual presence, teleconference systems, tele-teaching, telemedicine and ASP services to enterprises can make the prospect of moving outside metropolitan areas more attractive to an increasing group of citizens and enterprises. In these areas, they will find cheaper real estate prices, better social security conditions, higher landscape and environmental quality.

We have repeatedly highlighted that in a society that is increasingly oriented towards service production, the use of information and com-

munication technologies can no longer be considered an optional but, on the contrary, has become an indispensable prerequisite for territorial development and competitiveness. This implies of course that public authorities should adopt a proactive role in defining strategies for the development of digital networks. It is not about replacing private providers of connectivity services, but about endorsing the territorial development of adequate telecommunication networks (and the services that they can provide) by coordinating specific co-financing projects involving both public and private stakeholders. This requires a background of well-defined priorities based on policies that aim to restore territorial balance.

The resulting strategic framework is a set of intelligent territories made up of networks, where every hub is a crossing and switching point for multiple networks[81]: not only for road, rail and air connections, but also for telecommunication and digital networks.

Based on those considerations, let us try to identify, by way of example, some project initiatives that could be implemented in "intelligent" territories.

(81) see Veltz P., "Mondialisation. Villes et territories", Universitaires de France Press, Paris 1996

INTELLIGENT TERRITORIES

PROJECT INITIATIVES	QUALITY CRITERIA
1. Intelligent territorial planning	
1.1 Digital Network	Providing telecommunication networks capable of ensuring broadband internet access all over the territory in question. Mixed systems are possible, adjusting different technologies to territorial specificities: copper or optic fibre cable systems, wireless systems using radio frequencies (WiFi, WiMax, Hiperlan), satellite connections, digital terrestrial television, third generation UMTS telephony.
1.2 Infrastructure	Providing "intelligent" infrastructures capable of reacting to external inputs and providing services to users. Road infrastructures, for instance, can provide drivers with information, enabling them to change their travel plans. Thanks to an appropriate system of sensors, they can also assist drivers in difficult situations: impending dangers, extreme weather conditions, speed limit excess, etc.
1.3 Hot spot	These are areas providing internet access through a wireless connection (generally free of charge). In many cities, it is already possible to find hotspots in restaurants, train stations, airports, libraries, hotels and universities. It would also be useful to provide public hotspots outdoors, in parks, squares or in places that are generally used for entertainment or shopping, such as shopping malls.
2. Obtaining intelligent information from territories	
2.1 Nature monitoring	Systems of sensors and video-cameras can monitor various natural phenomena and activate adequate safety procedures accordingly. They can monitor water levels in water basins or dams, forest sectors for prompt intervention in case of fire, landslide risks in mountain slopes, snowfall levels in ski resorts, leakages in water pipes, etc.
2.2 City monitoring	Systems of sensors and video-cameras can ensure various monitoring actions in urban areas. For instance: the level of air and water purity, heat loss from buildings for a differentiated taxation system, traffic and availability of parking space in central areas, etc. Sensitive areas can also be monitored for safety reasons to ensure prompt intervention of police forces.
2.3 Info point	All the collected information can then be processed, selected and sent to users through mobile devices (palmtops, smart phones, i-pod, GPS, personal computers) or through info points strategically located around the city. Useful information can concern traffic and parking space, waiting time at the stops of public means of transport, availability of hotels and restaurants, bookings, etc.

PROJECT INITIATIVES	QUALITY CRITERIA
3. Planning intelligent applications for territories	
3.1 Telemedicine	Telemedicine is the combination of medical and IT techniques allowing for the provision of health services from a distance. It is possible to diagnose a patient who is not physically in the same room as the doctor through the remote transmission of data produced by diagnostic equipment. The most common telemedicine practices are: telepathology, teleradiology, telecardiology, teledermatology, telerehabilitation
3.2 E-government	E-government is the process of computerisation of public administration, allowing for documents to be processed and for procedures to be managed through digital systems, using ICTs, in order to streamline the workload of authorities and provide users (citizens and companies) with faster and more innovative services through, for instance, public authorities' websites.
3.3 Outsourcing	Delegating specific phases of the business production process (especially in SMEs) to external companies in order to limit costs and ensure adequate quality standards. Many of these services can be carried out on-line, through digital networks. Typically outsourced on-line services include: server housing and hosting, graphic services, call centres, management of administrative secretariats, etc.
4. Intelligent use of territories	
4.1 Marginal areas	Implementation of policies involving both public and private investments aimed at boosting the spread of telecommunication networks and the on-line services that they can provide in territories characterised by weak economies. The goal is to typify such territories as areas endowed with a high environmental and landscape value, coupled with an intense provision of high profile digital infrastructures and technological services.
4.2 Junction areas	These territories attract most of the mobilisation and integration efforts of public and private investments in order to improve infrastructural networks: not only air, maritime, rail and road connections with the corresponding logistic equipment, but also broadband digital networks integrated with centres of excellence for scientific and technological research and with cultural and financial networks.
4.3 Energy network	Energy networks allowing enterprises and individual users to produce renewable energy autonomously and exchange it when necessary. Intelligent meters enabling users to buy and sell energy automatically. Software capable of communicating real-time consumption of energy and re-directing energy flows during production peaks or slowdowns.
4.4 Refuse cycle	Recovery of energy from the refuse cycle. This can be produced either by waste-to-energy processes or by re-cycling (with consequent energy savings resulting from the non-production of materials, i.e. plastic, glass, etc.). Proper selective waste collection and proper re-cycling, using the most updated methodologies and state-of-the-art waste-to-energy procedures, can turn the refuse cycle into an economic as well as an environmental resource.

In order to conclude the reasoning that we have developed so far, we should now try to respond to the three initial questions that represented the introduction to this book.

« *Can digital networks determine territorial settlement patterns, thus playing the role which was previously exerted by other network infrastructures, such as the rail or the motorway system?* »

The answer can only be affirmative: digital networks will certainly determine future territorial settlement patterns! In a society where service production and knowledge value will acquire an increasingly strategic role, the use of information and communication technologies becomes an indispensable prerequisite. Perhaps, it is surprising to realise that this applies not only to "strong" territories, cities and metropolitan areas that are well integrated in global excellence systems, but also to weaker territories that see ICTs as an instrument for their emancipation. One of the side effects of globalisation is the widening of the gap between the territories that are involved in it and those which are excluded from it. As in the metaphor of "territorial layers" used in a previous chapter, digital networks represent the connecting threads between the local and global level, the systems allowing extensive global flows to be intercepted and turned into local territorial values.

« *Can the widespread use of ICT technologies contribute to the innovation of projects for territorial and urban transformation?* »

New technologies can indeed provide designers, administrators and technicians even with highly sophisticated applications that are capable of contributing to the innovation of urban instruments. We have demonstrated that, in some cases, ICTs can contribute to the innovation of existing methodologies and, in some other cases, they enable operations which were not possible beforehand. Anyway, it is an absolute fact that today, in the context of territorial planning, information and communication technologies are used in limited way in the face of their full potential. The consolidation of new methodologies and new instruments is hindered by a certain inertia which still seems to exist. But it is not a question of scepticism, it is rather a generational issue. When the younger generations of the "digital revolution", SMS, i-pod and video-games are fully integrated in the working population, Digital Urban Planning is likely to become the standard planning methodology.

« *Can the widespread use of digital networks, in the long term, give rise to new urban models or even new land management schemes?* »

The authors mentioned in the third and last part of this book predict a digital future pervaded by a daily use of technologies. We can hardly believe that this will not induce considerable changes in relationships and individual behaviours. And we can hardly believe that these changes will not give rise to new urban models and new territorial management schemes.t We tried to demonstrate this when we talked about "fragmentation and reassembling" of existing urban models. We have to admit, however, that in the past we have often believed that technological discoveries could bring about astonishing changes in the short term. Like the flying saucers in the extraordinary representations of cities by F.L. Wright. But this is not really the case. New models will result from the slow transformation of existing ones. There will be no sudden and traumatic changes. The transformation will be "soft". This is why the digital competences of new generations will play a determining role, just like their sensitivity towards eco-environmental issues.

This makes us see the future through rose-coloured glasses.

I have talked at length about this research paper with Alberto Clementi and Pepe Barbieri and I must thank them for their important suggestions on its structure. The meetings organised with the PRIN research group of the Department for Environment, Networks and Territory of the Faculty of Architecture in Pescara were also enriching. I am also very grateful to Franco Cuccurullo, Chacellor of the Università G. d'Annunzio, and to Fabio Capani, Chancellor of the Università Telematica Leonardo da Vinci, who have always supported me throughout these years. Finally, a special acknowledgment goes to Marco Petrella, who has dealt with all the administrative issues, Emanuela Ettorre, for her patient proofreading exercise, Pino Scaglione for taking care of the editorial part, Aldo Casciana for the general support given to this piece of work and Stefania Tieri for her choice of images.

sense*able* city lab:.:

MONOGRAPHIC INSERT:
SENSEable City – MIT Laboratory

edited by E. Morello, A.Biderman, F.M. Rojas, C. Ratti

This appendix summarises some recent studies carried
out by the Senseable City Lab, within the Massachusetts
Institute of Technology, Boston. The Senseable City Lab is
a research group, somewhere between the "Media Lab" and
the department of "Urban Studies and Planning", which set
out to understand how new technologies can change the way
in which we describe, understand, use and plan the city of
the future.

Situated at the intersection of architecture, urban planning, sociology, and human computer interaction, the MIT senseable city lab addresses the relationship between people, cities and new technologies. This piece is the Lab's first compendium of projects. Here we illustrate some of the core themes discussed in this book providing examples from our previous and ongoing projects.

Remember 1995? While just over a decade ago, it now feels like the distant past... Mosaic had just appeared as the first Internet browser. The Internet was in its infancy, still a secluded realm for geeky adepts. But so great was the excitement about the digital world that some people believed we would soon be living virtual lives. Scholars speculated about the impact of the ongoing digital revolution on the viability of cities. The mainstream view was that the `death of distance` as enabled by digital media and the Internet would certainly cause the `death of cities`. Gilder proclaimed that "Cities are leftover baggage from the industrial era" and concluded that "we are headed for the death of cities", due to the continued growth of personal computing, telecommunications, and distributed production. At the same time, Negroponte wrote in Being Digital that "[T]he post-information age will remove the limitations of geography. Digital living will include less and less dependence upon being in a specific place at a specific time, and the transmission of place itself will start to become possible."

With hindsight we all know that the story turned out quite differently. In fact, cities have never prospered as much as they have over the past couple of decades. China is currently on the road to building more urban fabric than has ever been built by humanity. And a particularly noteworthy moment occurred in 2008: for the first time in history more than half the world's population, 3.3 billion people, live in urban areas. By 2030, this figure is expected to reach almost 5 billion. The digital revolution did not end up killing our cities, but neither did it leave them unaffected. A layer of networked digital elements has blanketed our environment thus lending our cities a new layer of functionality. Sensors, cameras, and microcontrollers are used ever more extensively to manage city infrastructure, optimize transportation, monitor the environment, and to run security applications. Advances in microelectronics now make it possible to spread `smart dust` – networks of tiny wireless microelectromechanical systems (MEMS) sensors, robots, or devices. Most noticeable is the explosion in mobile phone use around the globe. More than 3.5 billion cell phones were in use worldwide in 2007. Across socio economic classes and throughout the five continents, mobile phones are ubiquitous.

All together, these digital objects and networks form an infrastructure that allows us to extract and insert information almost anywhere in the city, and in real-time. Processing this information and making it publicly accessible can enable people to make better decisions about the use of urban resources, mobility, and social interaction. This "feedback loop" of digital sensing and processing can begin to influence various complex and dynamic aspects of the city, improving the economic, social, and environmental sustainability of the places we inhabit. For example, an automated trip planner that relies on real-time information about bus, train, and taxi location, as well as congestion and pollution levels can help transit riders not only find the fastest travel route that matches their budget, but which also has the least impact on air quality.

Such rich information can be captured and transmitted not only through ambient sensors and computers embedded in the urban environment. Through personal digital devices such as mobile phones, people themselves can become probes, reporting on what is happening around them by intelligently harnessing the processing power and bandwidth they carry almost everywhere they go. As a result, our experience of urban spaces is transformed: it is no longer predominantly city designers and developers who give shape to our urban spaces, but almost anyone can participate in forming the digital layer of our environment. In short, the physical design and experience of the near-future city is intimately bound to the harnessing and transmission of digital information.

Research at the Senseable City Lab focuses on developing technologies that can mediate between physical urban space and the layers of digital flows produced by everyday urban functions, and on analyzing the changes our cities undergo due to this new coupling with digital technologies. Through our projects to date, we have explored areas such as interactive urban furniture, methods for data-fusion, pervasive data-mining, real-time data visualization, and more. This is possible because we consciously integrate aspects of urban studies, architecture, engineering, interaction design, computer science and social science. As such, in the five years since its founding, the Lab has grown into a multi-disciplinary group of over 20 people. The rich and conducive intellectual environment at MIT allows the Lab to bring together researchers with all of these different backgrounds and thus create a lively and productive exchange of ideas. Our group includes architects, graphic designers, urban planners, computer and electrical engineers, physicists, mathematicians, and social scientists representing over ten different nationalities. It is indeed a global, 21st century endeavor. With cities increasingly eager to experiment with the adoption of new technologies, a unique opportunity exists to transfer research out of the lab and into real urban environments for testing. With this in mind, the Lab has begun to carry out projects through partnerships with city administrations and members of industry. We have established the senseable city consortium, which brings our city and industry partners together with MIT researchers to share a vision, develop technologies, and deploy projects. This consortium also presents an opportunity for our partners to exchange information and ideas with each other, and to test possible future collaborations in a low-risk environment. As an example, the Lab has worked with the metropolitan planners of Copenhagen, Florence, Rome, New York, and Amsterdam in concert with industry partners such as Volkswagen-Audi, AT&T, Telecom Italia, and Mediaset.

Our approach to projects includes several phases, beginning with a vision for an urban future, or "urban demo", including the development of mediating technologies that could support the vision. This vision, tailored to a city's needs, can be motivated by the urban challenges a place may be confronting, or by opportunities for providing new experiences or services due to advances in digital technologies. For example, in the Real Time Rome project we created a visualization that overlaid information about the location of pedestrians and public transportation vehicles in real-time, thereby stipulating the potential for individuals to make efficient and informed decisions about their urban mobility.

Our urban demos are showcased at large public events and exhibitions in order to engage a cross-section of city users, public administrators, and industry representatives, who have the possibility of further developing, implementing and using the urban futures we envision. As an example, to realize the Real Time Rome project, the Lab partnered with Telecom Italia, the largest mobile phone service provider in Italy, ATAC, Rome's bus service operator, and Samarcanda Taxi. These urban infrastructure operators provided the aggregated, real-time information needed to illustrate the scale of urban activity supplied by their networks. The Lab then processed and presented this data in a series of real-time maps, which were exhibited at the 2006 Venice Biennale of Architecture. Other Lab projects have been shown at the New York Museum of Modern Art, Graz Kunsthaus, Ars Electronica, and the Canadian Center for Architecture.

After the completion of an urban demo or exhibition, the Lab transitions to a phase of long term research, where, together with our academic colleagues and industry partners, we explore the key theoretical lessons and technological challenges behind each project. We also examine how the technologies we develop can help us better understand cities and influence their design. Over the past two years researchers at the lab have been analyzing the data used in the Real Time Rome visualizations. This work has yielded nearly 20 peer-reviewed publications in fields that vary from environmental and urban planning to pervasive computing. All told, our academic publications have made contributions to the fields of pervasive computing, human computer interaction, intelligent transportation systems, control systems, and urban planning.

We are very grateful to Paolo Fusero, Pino Scaglione and to ACTAR for the invitation to present our work in this book. Given the fast pace of growth and production at the Lab, this is the first opportunity we have had to assess our work with a reflective eye. To be sure, innovating in our understanding of the urban condition requires a highly interdisciplinary approach to research. Our goal is not only to design, but to predict what may be the greatest needs and opportunities our cities face as they evolve alongside technology. We illustrate solutions that may be out of reach of technology at the moment, and work with our colleagues towards developing the scientific grounding for their realization.

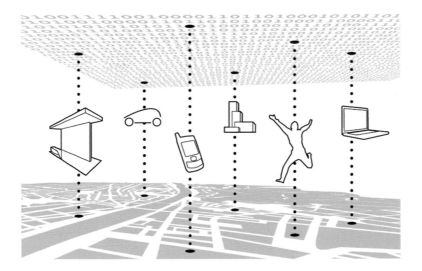

The works presented here are the result of a collaborative effort. Individual credits are given in the text that describes each project. Below is a list of all the people who have been involved with the SENSEable City Lab since its inception:

Researchers
Carlo Ratti (Director), Assaf Biderman (Associate Director), Francesco Calabrese, Filippo Dal Fiore, Fabien Girardin, Gabriel Grise, Liang Liu, Eugenio Morello, Nashid Nabian, Bernd Resch, Jon Reades, Christine Outram, Francisca Rojas, Andres Sevtsuk, Andrea Vaccari

Past Researchers
Burak Arikan, Daniel Berry, Enrico Costanza, Talia Dorsey, Sarah Dunbar, Chris Fematt, Lucie Boyce Flather, Saba Ghole, Daniel Gutierrez, Guy Hoffman, Sonya Huang, Kristian Kloeckl, Sriram Krishnan, Xiongjiu Liao, David Lee, Alyson Liss, Jia Lou, Andrea Mattiello, Justin Moe, James Patten, Riccardo Pulselli, Pietro Pusceddu, François Proulx, Martin Ramos, Susanne Seitinger, Najeeb Marc Tarazi, Kenny Verbeeck, Yao Wang, Sarah Williams

References
Castells, M. (1996). The Rise of the Network Society (2nd ed., Vol. I). Oxford UK Malden MA: Blackwell.
Gilder, G. (1995). Forbes. ASAP, 27 (56).
Negroponte, Nicholas. (1995). Being Digital. New York: Knopf UNFPA. (2007). State of World Population 2007. Retrieved October 30, 2008, from http://www.unfpa.org/swp/2007/english/introduction.html
The World Factbook https://www.cia.gov/library/publications/the-world-factbook/rankorder/2151rank.html.

Programmable Window I SENSEable City Laboratory with Tangible Media Group,
MIT Media Lab, 2004
Team: Carlo Ratti, lab director; Assaf Biderman, Martin Ramos

A huge electronic display on a skyscraper facade can be interesting to passing
pedestrians, but if you are inside the building it simply blocks your view of the
street. The joint project between MIT's Media Laboratory and the Department of
Urban Studies and Planning develops a transparent display that does not entirely
block incoming light.

The research group is adapting a commercially available film used in electronic window shades, a high-tech alternative to blinds or curtains that lightens and darkens
when electricity is applied and removed. The display is a matrix of small separate
pieces of the film. A grid of tiny wires connects the pieces to a computer, which can
compose letters and figures in grayscale patterns. Because the film at its darkest
blocks only 40 percent of incoming light, and because only some of the pieces in
the matrix are darkened at any given time, people sitting behind the display can
still see outside.

1I Rendering of the Programmable Window

iSpots I SENSEable City Laboratory, 2005
Team Members: Carlo Ratti, group director; Andres Sevtsuk, coordinator; Sonya Huang, Daniel
Gutierrez, Justin Moe, David Lee, Xiongjiu Liao, Jia Lou

While many cities have proposed plans to install wireless Internet nodes (wi-fi) on every street lamp, MIT has activated 2,800 access points on its university campus, completing full coverage on October 2005. The effects of complete wireless coverage are monumental, as traditional work spaces are being abandoned in favor of more flexible environments such as lounges, cafes and public spaces.
The iSPOTS project documents these changes in real time using log information from MIT's wireless network.
The iSPOTS project aims at describing changes in living and working at MIT by mapping the dynamics
of the wireless network in real-time. Thus, the complex and dispersed individual movement patterns that make up the daily life of the campus are revealed, helping to answer many questions: Which physical spaces are preferred for work by the MIT community? How could future physical planning of the campus suit the community's changing needs? Which location-based services would be most helpful for students and academics?
Also, as many cities around the world are launching extensive wireless initiatives, the analysis of the MIT environment could provide valuable insights for the future. Will today's MIT be tomorrow's urban experience?

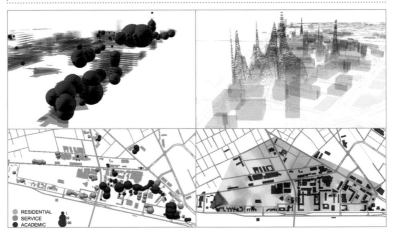

RESIDENTIAL
SERVICE
ACADEMIC

1| Total number of WLAN users. The bubbles represent the intensity of traffic.
2| 3-D visualization showing the WLAN traffic intensity on the campus.
3| Interpolated representation of WLAN usage at a given time.
4| Interpolated representation of WLAN usage at a given time.

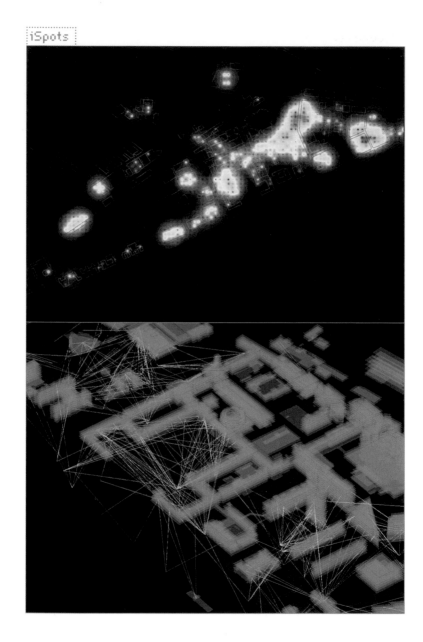

5| Map showing the WLAN traffic intensity on the campus.
6| 3-D visualization showing the sniffing of WLAN traffic on the campus.

Mobile Landscape Graz I SENSEable City Laboratory, 2005
The project was shown at the M-City exhibition (curator: Marco De Michelis),
Kunsthaus Graz; Oct 01, 2005 - Jan 08, 2006.
Team Members: Carlo Ratti, group director; Daniel Berry, Andrea Mattiello,
Eugenio Morello, Andres Sevtsuk
Design team: David Lee, Xiongjiu Liao, Jia Lou, Sonya Y Huang, Daniel A Gutierrez
In collaboration with A1 - Mobilkom Austria

Mobile Landscape Graz harnesses the potential of mobile phones as an affordable,
ready-made, and ubiquitous medium that allows the city to be sensed and displayed
in real-time as a complex, pulsating entity. Because it is possible to simultaneously
"ping" the cell phones of thousands of users -thereby establishing their location
in space at a given moment in time -these devices can be used as a highly dynamic
tracking tool that describes how the city is used and transformed by its citizens.
The polis is thus interpreted as a shifting entity formed by dynamic webs of human
interactions in space-time, rather than simply as a fixed, physical environment.
Previous initiatives, notably Laura Kurgan's "You Are Here: Museu" (1996) and
the Waag Society's "Amsterdam Real-Time" (2002) initiated this process by ex-
ploring the qualities and potential of GPS technology. Mobile Landscape builds
on and expands these efforts by using cell phone technology, for the first time,
to radically increase the interactive capacity and number of users involved in the
mapping of the city. Mobile Landscape (re)presents urban flux simultaneously in
the Kunsthaus Graz and in a publicly accessible website.

1l visualization of traffic migration (handovers) in the City of Graz.

138

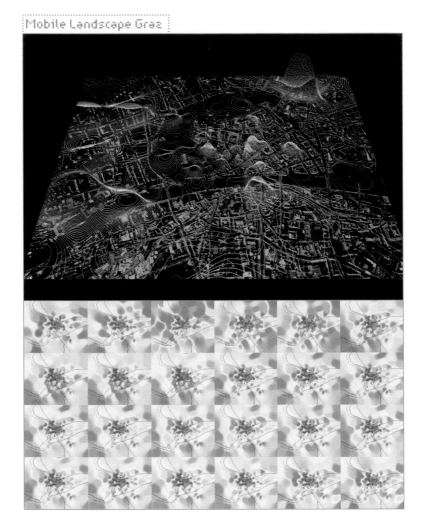

2| 3-D Visualization of cell-phone traffic intensity superimposed on the city of Graz.
3| This map shows cell-phone traffic intensity (measured in Erlang) during a period of 24 hours.

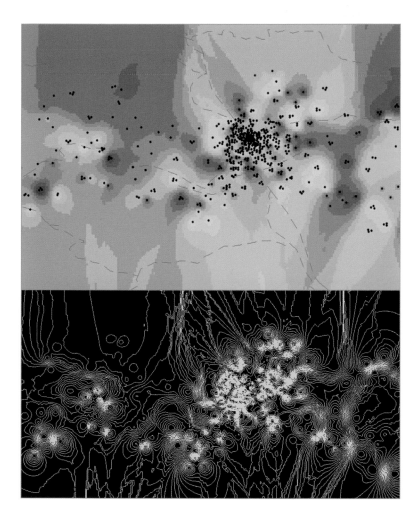

4I Traffic intensity visualization in the city of Graz. Black dots represent the cell-phone towers.
5I Traffic intensity visualization in the city of Graz.

The Adaptable Bus Stop I SENSEable City Laboratory, 2006
The project was shown at the 2006 Venice Biennale, directed by Professor Richard
Burdett. Sep 10, 2006 - Nov 19, 2006.
Team Members: Carlo Ratti, group director; Assaf Biderman, project leader design:
Kenny Verbeeck, Alyson Liss, Lucie Boyce Flather, James Patten, interaction
design
collaboration: Kenneth Namkung, Guy Hoffman, Andres Sevtsuk
web site : Sarah Dunbar,
Partners: City of Zaragoza, Spain; TUZSA -Zaragoza Busses

The city of Zaragoza, Spain partnered with MIT's SENSEable City Lab to design
an interactive bus stop. As host to the 2008 World Expo, the city planned to install a new bus service. The Lab's design for the Adaptable Bus Stop incorporates
several types of digital technologies in order to offer new services to the public,
allow for cost-effective manufacturing, and enable the generation of advertising
revenue.
A parametric design model determines a unique design for each stop providing
optimal sheltering at minimal cost. Bus riders can plan their trip on a interactive
map, exchange relevant community information on a digital message board, surf
the web, and use the digital media on the bus shelter as an interface with their
mobile devices.

1I Interacting with the bus stop

2| Bus Stop prototype shown at the 2006 Venice Biennale
3| Bus Stop computer rendering
4| Interactive trip planning map
5| Zaragoza bus stop poster shown at 2006 Venice Biennale
6| Bus Stop roof designed with Zaragoza local patterns

Real Time Rome I SENSEable City Laboratory, 2006
The project was shown at the 2006 Venice Biennale, directed by Professor Richard
Burdett. Sep 10, 2006 - Nov 19, 2006.
Team Members: Carlo Ratti, group director; Andres Sevtsuk, curator; Burak Ari-
kan, Assaf Biderman, Francesco Calabrese, Filippo Dal Fiore, Saba Ghole, Daniel
Gutierrez, Sonya Huang, Sriram Krishnan, Justin Moe, Francisca Rojas, Najeeb
Marc Tarazi,
Principal Sponsor: Telecom Italia,
Partners: Biennale di Venezia, City of Rome, Google, ATAC -Rome Buses, Samar-
canda Taxi I Microtek

The visualizations of Real Time Rome synthesize data from various real-time networks to understand patterns of daily life in Rome. We interpolate the aggregate
mobility of people according to their mobile phone usage and visualize it synchro-
nously with the flux of public transit, pedestrians, and vehicular traffic. By over-
laying mobility information on geographic and socio-economic references of Rome
we unveil the relationships between fixed and fluid urban elements. These real-
time maps help us understand how neighborhoods are used in the course of a day,
how the distribution of buses and taxis correlates with densities of pedestrians,
how goods and services are distributed in the city, or how different social groups,
such as tourists and residents, inhabit the city. With the resulting visualizations
users can interpret and react to the shifting urban environment.

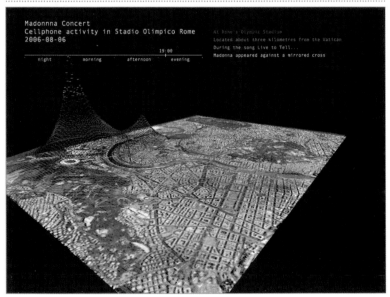

Madonnna Concert
Cellphone activity in Stadio Olimpico Rome
2006-08-06

At Rome's Olympic Stadium
Located about three kilometres from the Vatican
During the song Live to Tell...
Madonna appeared against a mirrored cross

19:00

night   morning   afternoon   evening

1I Average cellphone users distribution on the satellite image of the city of Rome just beofre Madonna's concert on 6 August 2006 @ 7pm (black and white). A large crowd is assembling around the
Olympic Stadium

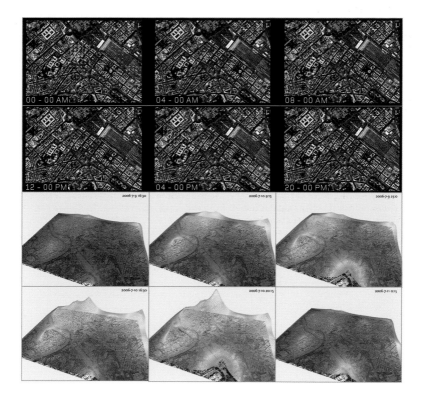

2| The movement dynamics of cellular phone users at different times of a day in district scale. Area around the Basilica di Santa Maria Maggiore

3| Final match, World Cup 2006. Average cellphone users distribution on the satellite image of the city of Rome. The final match of the World Cup 2006 was played on July 9th, from 8 to 10 pm approximately. Afterwards, people started celebrating around the Circo Massimo in Rome, shown in the image. The following day the Italian winning team arrived in Rome and celebrations continued from the afternoon till morning

Tracing the Visitor's Eye I SENSEable City Laboratory, 2007
Team Members: Carlo Ratti, group director; Fabien Girardin, project idea and
research; Filippo Dal Fiore, definition of research needs with local partnersFoun-
ding Partner: Provincia Firenze
Technical Partner: APT Firenze (Agency for the Promotion of Tourism)

Analyzing the archives of human-generated, spatiotemporal data can reveal high-
level behavioral information valuable to urban planners, traffic engineers, and
tourism authorities. In Tracing the Visitor's Eye, we collect and visualize the physical presence over time of tourists from the digital footprints they make available
to the public via their postings of photographs on the Internet.
The process of recording and collecting the data takes place as follows: First,
tourists take photos during their travels. Later, they associate a geographical location to their photos through a map interface in Flickr or other external map-based
services. Some tech savvy users have their photos geographically annotated with
location data collected by GPS devices embedded or external to their cameras.
Via the Flickr API, we are able to retrieve the coordinates, time stamp, accuracy
level, and an obfuscated identifier of the owner of the publicly available photos
within a given area. The collected data allows us to create an overview of tourist
movement and photographic interest at various geographical scales.

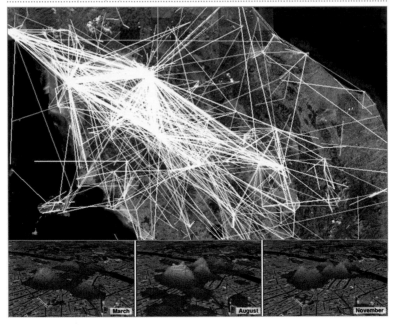

1I Movements of tourists in northern part of central Italy.
2I Screenshots of the spatio-temporal animation of the presence of tourists in downtown Florence in
2007. Photographic imagery copyright 2007 DigitalGlobe.

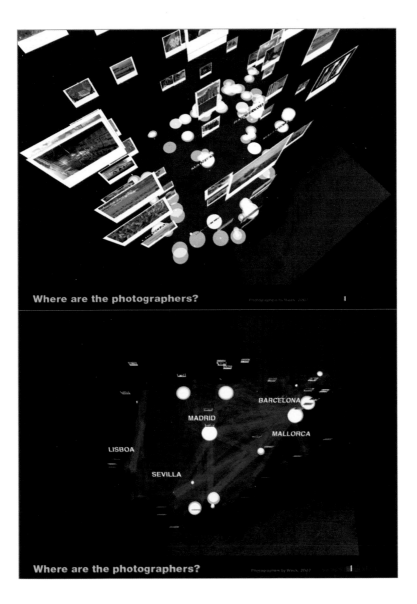

3| Visualization showing the localization of photographers in the Iberian Peninsula during a week in 2007.
4| Visualization showing the localization of photographers in the Iberian Peninsula during a week in 2007.

Wiki City Rome I SENSEable City Laboratory, 2007
The project was shown at the 2007 Notte Bianca in Rome. Sep 08, 2007
Team Members: Carlo Ratti, group director; Assaf Biderman, Francesco Calabrese,
team leader, Fabien Girardin, Kristian Kloeckl, team leader, Bernd Resch
Founding Partners: Pagine Gialle, Telecom Italia, Telespazio
Technical Partners: La Repubblica, ATAC -Rome Buses, Trenitalia

Rome's Notte Bianca festival is all about the city, the people and the all-night
events. How are people moving throughout Rome to experience this exceptional
night of city-wide activities and events? The Wiki City Rome visualizations were
projected live onto a large public screen during the night of September 8th 2007
in Rome.
The visualizations overlaid various types of data in real time onto a map of the
city. Events happening around the city showed up on the map in their corresponding
locations at the time they occurred; a color overlay used cell phone activity data
to illustrate how Romans moved within the city. This captured people moving in
the city by foot. Wiki City Rome also illustrated other forms of mobility during the
Notte Bianca by showing the position of Rome's buses in real time. This allowed
spectators to know whether buses where in their vicinity at a given point in time
and whether the supply of buses coincided with pedestrian demand.

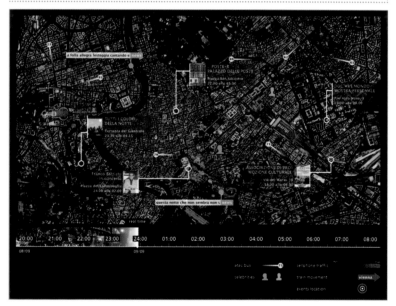

1I A detail of the interface of WickiCity Rome.

21 31 The public venue where the WickiCity Rome interface was shown.

Copencycle

Copencycle| SENSEable City Laboratory, 2008
Project Team: Carlo Ratti, group director; Christine Outram, Project Leader; Assaf
Biderman, Assistant Director; Francesco Calabrese, Mauro Martino, Michael Lin
Additional Collaborators: Benjamin Waber, Vasilena Vasilev, Brian Yang, Smart
Cities Group, MIT Media Laboratory
Research Advisor: William J Mitchell
Partners: Kobenhavns Kommune

CopenCycle explores the use of real time technologies to map the flow of people
and urban resources in Copenhagen to better understand urban dynamics in real
time. By revealing the pulse of the city, the project aims to show how technology
can help individuals and the city's planning institutions to make more informed
decisions about their environment and resources with a special emphasis on people's use of public spaces.

In the long run, the project seeks to integrate mobile and digital technologies to
produce more detailed studies of bicycle movement and the services and routes
needed to maintain a sustainable urban transportation system.

1| Climate Summit Choice Exchange application. Map of the bike congestional level.
2| Climate Summit Choice Exchange application. Diagram with the Kilometers cycled during the year
3| Climate Summit Smart Helmet with embedded camera.

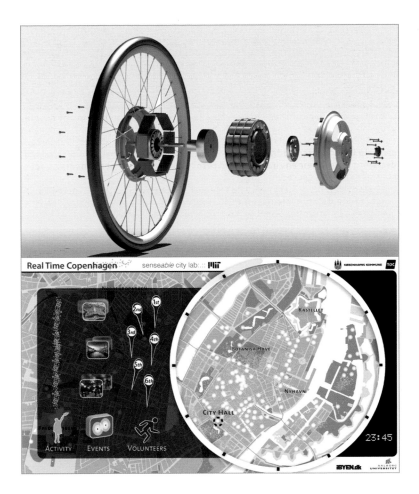

4| Climate Summit Green Wheel project. Exploded image of rear wheel of prototype hybrid smart bicycle. Battery, motor and electronics are all packed in the rear wheel.
5| The interface of Real Time Copenhagen displayed on the evening of the culture night, October 2008.

Digital Water Pavillon I carlorattiassociati -walter nicolino & carlo ratti ,2008
BOSTON: Interactive water wall concept_MIT MEDIA LABORATORY / SMART
CITIES GROUP; Digital Mile design_MIT DEPARTMENT OF URBAN STUDIES AND
PLANNING / CITY DESIGN AND DEVELOPMENT GROUP; Expo gateway prelimina-
ry design_MIT SENSEABLE CITY LAB
TORINO: Architectural Design_CARLORATTIASSOCIATI
ZARAGOZA: Client_CITY OF ZARAGOZA; EXPOAGUA ZARAGOZA 2008
PARIS: Landscape architecture_AGENCE TER
MILANO: Graphic design_STUDIO FM MILANO
MADRID: Engineering_ARUP; Interactive water wall engineering_LUMIARTEC-
NIA INTERNATIONAL; Lead contractor_SIEMENS; Site supervision_TYPSA;

The Digital Water Pavilion is a singular and innovative project along the Milla
Digital, implemented by Expoagua Zaragoza 2008 on behalf of the City of Zaragoza,
Spain. Located where the Expo site meets the Milla Digital area, the DWP brings
together the themes of water and digital technologies. The minimalist expression
of the Digital Water Pavilion is at the same time: a sophisticated machine of high
mechanical precision; a building that appears and disappears through a hydraulic
pistons system; and a flexible space, that changes and responds via 120 meters of
water walls controlled digitally by almost 3.000 electromagnetic valves.
The valves can be opened and closed, at high frequency, via computerized controls.
This produces a curtain of falling water with gaps at specified points - a pattern
of pixels created from air and water instead of illuminated points on a screen.
The entire surface becomes a one-bit-deep digital display continuously scrolling
downwards. Something like an inkjet printer on a huge scale. So, how to make really
fluid, reconfigurable architecture? The Digital Water Pavilion aims to stand as a
possible answer to that endeavor. Fluid in the literal sense of the word. But also
fluid as a reconfigurable, responsive building. The difference between wall and
door can disappear.

1l Rendering of the digital water pavilion. carlorattiassociati - walter nicolino & carlo ratti

21 31 Rendering of the digital water pavilion. carlorattiassociati – walter nicolino & carlo ratti

4| Pictures taken at the inauguration of the DWP in June 2008. Guy Hoffman
5| Pictures taken at the inauguration of the DWP in June 2008. Ramak Fazel
6| Pictures taken at the inauguration of the DWP in June 2008. Guy Hoffman

71 Pictures taken at the inauguration of the DWP in June 2008. Max Tomasinelli (www.maxtomasinelli.com)

New York Talk Exchange I SENSEable City Laboratory, 2008
The project was shown at the Design and the Elastic Mind exhibition (curator: Pa-
ola Antonelli), the Museum of Modern Art, New York. Feb 24, 2008 – May 12, 2008.
Team Members: Carlo Ratti, group director; Kristian Kloeckl, project leader; Assaf
Biderman, Francesco Calabrese, Margaret Ellen Haller, Aaron Koblin, Francisca
Rojas, Andrea Vaccari
Research Advisors: William Mitchell, Saskia Sassen
at&t labs research: Alexandre Gerber, Chris Rath, Michael Merritt, Jim Rowland
Project Sponsors: at&t
Technical Partners: Yahoo, design innovation team, BT under the patronage of:
The Italian Cultural Institute of New York

New York Talk Exchange illustrates the global exchange of information in real time
by visualizing volumes of long distance telephone and IP (Internet Protocol) data
flowing between New York and cities around the world. In an information age, telecommunications such as the Internet and the telephone bind people across space
by eviscerating the constraints of distance. To reveal the relationships that New
Yorkers have with the rest of the world, New York Talk Exchange asks: How does
the city of New York connect to other cities? With which cities does New York have
the strongest ties and how do these relationships shift with time? How does the
rest of the world reach into the neighborhoods of New York?

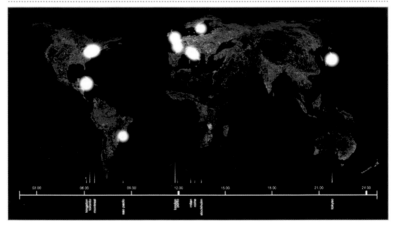

1l Pulse of the planet. Time zones influence the global rhythm of communications. Pulse of the Planet
illustrates the volume of international calls between New York City and 255 countries over the
twenty-four hours in a day. Areas of the world receiving and making fewer phone calls shrink while
areas experiencing a greater amount of voice call activity expand. International cities with the most
call activity to and from New York are highlighted according to time zone.

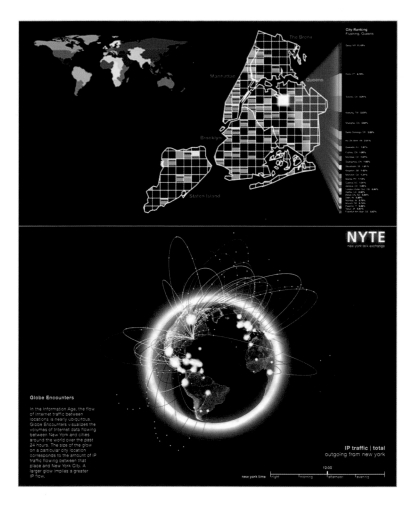

21 World Within New York. World Within New York shows how different New York neighborhoods reach out to the rest of the world via the AT&T telephone network. The city is divided into a grid of 2-kilometer square pixels where each pixel is colored according to the regions of the world wherein the top connecting cities are located. The widths of the color bars represent the proportion of world regions in contact with each neighborhood. Encoded within each pixel is also a list of the world cities that account for 70% of the communications with that particular area of New York.

31 Global Encounters. In the Information Age, the flow of IP (Internet Protocol) data between locations is nearly ubiquitous. Global Encounters visualizes in real time the volumes of Internet data flowing between New York and cities around the world. The size of the glow on a particular city location corresponds to the amount of IP traffic flowing between that place and New York City. A greater glow implies a greater IP flow.

Trash Track

Trash Track | SENSEable City Laboratory, 2008
The project will be exhibited at the Situated Technologies exhibition (curator: Mark Shepard), New York City. Sep 2009.
Team Members: Carlo Ratti, group director; Eugenio Morello, project leader; Assaf Biderman, Francesco Calabrese, Fabien Girardin, Christine Outram, Francisca Rojas
Research Advisors: Rex Britter, William Mitchell
Consultants: Caterina Ginzburg, Aaron Koblin, Armin Linke, Stephen Miles, Valerie M. Thomas
Project Sponsors: The Architectural League of New York

Trash Track uses smart tags attached to different types of garbage in order to track waste in real time as it traverses the city's sanitation system. The goals of Trash Track are to reveal the disposal process, or "removal chain", of our everyday objects and waste, and to highlight inefficiencies in today's recycling and sanitation systems. People in different neighborhoods throughout the city, ideally representing all five boroughs, are asked to install a total of 1000 wireless tracking devices on different types of waste products. The information produced by the Trash Track project helps to formulate more effective recycling policies and introduces a "supply chain" approach to waste management, which we call the "removal chain", as a reverse symmetrical system to the already existing delivery chain.

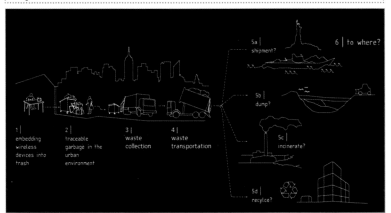

1| The waste flow in New York City.

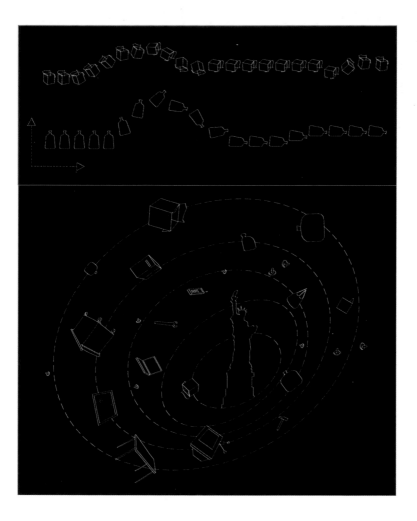

2| The diagram that shows how the object moves in space and time.
3| Trash in New York City.

Bibliography

* AA.VV., 2006, "Dieci anni di governo delle complessità del territorio", Ministry of Infrastructures and Transports - General Direction for Territorial Coordination, Rome.
* Anrong Dang, Huizhen S., Haoying H., Lei W., 2005, "Study on system of technical methods for digital urban planning", ISPRS Workshop on Service and Application of Data Infrastructure, XXXVI (4/W6), October 14-16, Hangzhou, China.
* Ashthon T.S., 1953, "La rivoluzione industriale", Laterza, Bari. (*The industrial revolution*)
* Aurigi A., 2005, "Making the Digital City", Ashgate, Hampshire England.
* Barbagallo C., 1951, "Le origini della grande industria contemporanea", La nuova Italia, Florence. (*The origins of the great contemporary industry*)
* Bauman Z., 2000, "Liquid Modernity", Polity Press, Cambridge.
* Benevolo L., 1984, "Le origini dell'urbanistica moderna", Laterza, Bari. (*The origins of modern urbanism*)
* Bonacina D., 2007, "Internet dalle origini al terzo millennio", working paper published on http://bonacina.wordpress.com (*Internet from its origins to the third millennium*)
* Caddy J., 2001, "Citizens as Partners: Information, Consultation and Public Participation in Policy-Making", OECD Publishing, Paris.
* Castells M., 2004, "La città delle reti", Marsilio, Venice. (*The city of networks*)
* Castells M., 2002, "The Information Society and the Welfare State: The Finnish Model". Oxford UP, Oxford.
* Castells M., 2004, "The Network Society: A Cross-Cultural Perspective". Cheltenham, UK; Northampton, MA, Edward Edgar ed.
* Castells M., 2006, "The Network Society: From Knowledge to Policy". Center for Transatlantic Relations ed.
* Cazes B., 2004, "La prospective: un objet vénérable aux nombreuses identités", in *Urbanisme*, n. 334.
* Clementi A., 2006, "Un avvenire possible del territorio italiano", in *Reti e territori al futuro*, Ministry of Infrastructures ed., Rome. (*A possible future for the Italian territory*)
* Clementi A., 2008, "Corridoi, piattaforme, città senza fine", in *Opere pubbliche e città adriatica*, AAVV, Actar-D List, Barcelona. (*Corridors, platforms, never-ending cities*)
* Crozet Y., Musso P., 2003, "Réseux, services et territoires". *Horizon 2020*, Datar, Editions de l'Aube, Paris.
* De Biase L., Meletti G. (edited by), 2001, "Bidone.com?", Fazi Editore, Milano.
* Della Porta D., 2004, "Comitati di cittadini e democrazia urbana", Rubettino ed., Catanzaro. (*Citizens committees and urban democracy*)
* Dematteis G., Clementi A., Palermo P.C., 1996, "Le forme del territorio italiano", Laterza, Bari-Roma. (*The shape of the Italian territory*)
* Duguid P., 2004, "The Social Life of Information", Harvard Business School Press, Harvard, Mass.
* Fistola R., 2001, "Nuovi strumenti urbanistici per il governo delle trasformazioni territoriali indotte dalle nuove tecnologie della comunicazione: il Piano Digitale", the *XXII Italian Conference on Regional Sciences*, AISRE, Venice. (*New urban planning tools for the management of territorial transformations brought about by new communication technologies: the Digital Plan*)
* Fistola R., 2006, "Digital urban planning e pianificazione digitale del territorio", in the *XXVII Italian Conference on Regional Sciences*, AISRE, Pisa. (*Digital urban planning and territorial urban planning*)
* Fontana G., 2006, "Reti e territori al futuro", Ministry of Infrastructures ed. Rome. (*Future networks and territories*)
* Fusero P., 2008, "E-planning: urbanistica e reti digitali", in: L. Sacchi, M. Unali, *Abitare Virtuale*, ed. Kappa, Rome. (*E-planning: urbanism and digital networks*)
* Fusero P., 2008, "Reti digitali e riqualificazione territoriale" in *Opere pubbliche e città adriatica*, AAVV, Actar-D List, Barcelona. (*Digital networks and territorial revitalisation*)
* Fusero P., 2004, "Il rapporto pubblico privato nel PRG: pratiche contesti e nuovi orizzonti", Palombi ed., Rome. (*The relationship between the public and the private sector in the General Town Planning Scheme: practises, contexts and new horizons*)
* Fusero P. (edited by), 2004, "Ecoscape: valorizzazione del patrimonio paesaggistico ed ambientale", Sala ed., Pescara. (*Ecoscape: enhancement of landscape and environmental heritage*)
* Granelli A. (edited by), 2005, "Comunicare l'innovazione. Perché il successo del nuovo dipende

dalla capacità di spiegarlo", ed. Il Sole 24 Ore, Milan. (*Communicating innovation. Because the success of innovations depends on the ability to explain them*)

* Indovina F., 1993, "Strategie e soggetti per la trasformazione urbana, anni '80", in F. Indovina (edited by) *La città occasionale*, F. Angeli, Milan. (*Strategies and stakeholders for urban transformation, the '80s*)

* Ishida T., 2002, "Understanding Digital Cities: Cross-Cultural Perspectives", MIT Press, Cambridge, MA.

* Ishida T., 2002, "Digital City Kioto", in *Communications of the ACM*, n. 7 vol.45

* Köhler Tyndall J., 2006, "Economics", in *Intelligent Infrastructure Futures Scenarios Toward 2055 – Perspective and Process*, UK Office of Science and Technology, London.

* Laguerre M. S., 2006, "The Digital City: The American Metropolis and Information Technology", Palgrave Macmillan, New York.

* Lamberti A., 2006, "Le strade in Itallia: dalle origini all'autostrada del Sole", working paper pubblicato su http://cronologia.leonardo.it. (*Italian roads: from the origins to the Autostrada del Sole*)

* Landrieu J., 2004, "*Quelle prospective?*", in *Urbanisme*, n. 334.

* Linturi R., Koivunen M. Sulkanen J., 2000, "Helsinki Arena 2000: augmenting a real city to a virtual one", in *Digital Cities: Experiences, Technologies and Future Perspectives*, Springer Verlag, New York.

* Mattelart A., 2001, "Histoire della societè de l'information", Einaudi, Turin, 2002. (Italian translation)

* Mitchell, W. J., 1995, "City of Bits: Space, Place and the Infobahn", MIT Press.

* Mitchell, W. J., 1999, "E-topia: Urban Life, Jim – But Not As We Know It", MIT Press.

* Mitchell, W. J., 2000, "Designing the Digital City", in: AAVV, *Digital City*, Springer Berlin, Berlin.

* Mitchell, W. J., 2003, "Me ++: The Cyborg Self and the Networked City", MIT Press.

* Osborn D., 2006, "Environmental implications", in *Intelligent Infrastructure Futures Scenarios Toward 2055 – Perspective and Process*, UK Office of Science and Technology ed., London.

* Stevens B., Shieb P.A., Andrieu M., 2006, "A cross- sectoral perspective on development of global infrastructures to 2030", in *Infrastructure to 2030*, OCDE ed., Paris.

* Stoll C., 1999, "High-Tech Heretic", Garzanti, Milan, 2001. (Italian translation)

* Subioli P., 2007, "Il ruolo della comunicazione nell'e-government", *Cronache dell'e-government*, http://www.cronache-egovernment.it. (*The role of communication in e-government*)

* Tully, A., 2006, "Foresight Intelligent Infrastructure Systems Project: Pervasive Tagging, Sensors and Data Collection", http://www.foresight.gov.uk/Previous _ Projects/Intelligent _ Infrastructure _ Systems/Reports _ and _ Publications/Intelligent _ Infrastructure _ Futures/ Reviews/Tagging _ Sensorsa.pdf

* Tutino A., 1986, "L'efficacia del Piano", Casa Città Territorio ed., Rome. (*The effectiveness of the Plan*)

* Urry J., 2006, "Social processes", in *Intelligent Infrastructure Futures Scenarios Toward 2055 – Perspective and Process*, UK Office of Science and Technology, London.

* Van den Besselaar P. Beckers D., 1998, "Demographics and Sociographics of the Digital City", Springer-Verlag, New York.

* Veltz P., 1996, "Mondialisation. Villes et territories", Universitaires de France Press, Paris.

* Weiser M., 1991, "The Computer for the 21st Century", in *Scientific American*, 265, September.

* Wu S. et al., 2001, "Digital Urban Planning, Concept and support technology", in Lai M. and Wang M., *Theory and Practice of Digital City*, World Book Press, Guangzhou.

* Zenezini M., 2006, "E' finita la New economy?", working paper n. 89 published by the Department of Economics and Statistics of the University of Trieste http://www.univ.trieste.it/~nirdses. (*Is the new economy over?*)

Edited by
LISt Laboratorio
Internazionale Editoriale
Barcelona (Spain)
www.listlab.eu
www.momboo.net
(in Italy: Trento-Roma)

Dart collection
Scientific board: Alberto Clementi
(coordinatore), Piercarlo Palermo
(Milano), Giuseppe Barbieri, (Pescara),
Giuliano Leone (Palermo), Alfonzo
Ruiz Braz (Oporto), Peter Gabrielcic
(Lubiana)
(printed with the contribution of Dart/
Pescara)

Collection I _ CARe
Italy Contemporary Advanced Research
Scientific board: Maurizio Carta
(Palermo), Alberto Cecchetto (Venezia),
Carlo Gasparrini (Napoli), Manuel Gausa
(Barcelona/Genova), José Luis Esteban
Penelas (Madrid), Mosè Ricci (Genova),
Pino Scaglione (Trento)

Author
Paolo Fusero
Final insert edited by
Senseable City Lab of Massachusetts
Institute of Technology (Boston)

Editorial coordination
Pino Scaglione

Art Direction
Massimiliano Scaglione

Graphic Design
Claudia Tagliabue

Translations
Stefania Contarino

Printing
S.A. de Litografia

ISBN 978-88-95623-06-1
DL B-15968-2009

Distribution
Actar D
Roca i Batlle, 2
08023 Barcelona
office@actar-d.com
www.actar-d.com

List is an editorial workshop, set in
Barcelona, works on the contemporary
issues. List not only publishes, but also
researches, proposes, endeawour,
promotes, produces, creates networks